A Da Capo Press Reprint Series

**FRANKLIN D. ROOSEVELT
AND THE ERA OF THE NEW DEAL**
GENERAL EDITOR: FRANK FREIDEL
Harvard University

THE TRANSIENT
UNEMPLOYED

Division of Research
Work Projects Administration

Research Monographs

Works Progress Administration
Division of Social Research
Research Monograph III

THE TRANSIENT UNEMPLOYED

A Description and Analysis of the Transient Relief Population

By John N. Webb

DA CAPO PRESS • NEW YORK • 1971

A Da Capo Press Reprint Edition

This Da Capo Press edition of *The Transient Unemployed* is an un-abridged republication of the first edition published in Washington, D.C., in 1935. It is reprinted by permission from a copy of the original edition owned by the Harvard College Library.

Library of Congress Catalog Card Number 71-166337
ISBN 0-306-70335-1

Published by Da Capo Press, Inc.
A Subsidiary of Plenum Publishing Corporation
227 West 17th Street, New York, N.Y. 10011
All Rights Reserved

Manufactured in the United States of America

1630580

THE TRANSIENT
UNEMPLOYED

WORKS PROGRESS ADMINISTRATION
DIVISION OF SOCIAL RESEARCH

THE TRANSIENT UNEMPLOYED

A Description and Analysis of the
Transient Relief Population

BY

JOHN N. WEBB

RESEARCH MONOGRAPH

III

WASHINGTON
1935

WORKS PROGRESS ADMINISTRATION

HARRY L. HOPKINS, *Administrator*

CORRINGTON GILL
Assistant Administrator

HOWARD B. MYERS, *Director*
Social Research Division

LETTER OF TRANSMITTAL

WORKS PROGRESS ADMINISTRATION

Washington, D.C., March 10, 1936

Sir:

I have the honor to transmit herewith a report dealing with problems of the transient unemployed as faced by the Transient Division of the Federal Emergency Relief Administration for the period beginning with the establishment of that Division and continuing through June 1935.

This report brings together the results of a series of studies conducted in the Division of Research, Statistics and Finance of the Federal Emergency Relief Administration, and presents an exhaustive analysis of the characteristics of the transient relief population, their movements, their reasons for migration, and the problems involved in the reabsorption of this group into private industrial employment.

This report was prepared by *John N. Webb,* under the supervision of *Henry B. Arthur,* Assistant Director, and the general direction of *Howard B. Myers,* Director, of the Division of Social Research, Works Progress Administration. Acknowledgement is made of the assistance rendered by many other individuals and departments who cooperated or contributed in the work of preparing this report.

CORRINGTON GILL
Assistant Administrator

Hon. HARRY L. HOPKINS
Works Progress Administrator

CONTENTS

CONTENTS

Text Tables

Charts

CONTENTS

CONTENTS

CONTENTS

CONTENTS   Page.

(Appendix C)

RESUMÉ

The transient relief population consisted of unattached individuals and family groups who were not legal residents of the community in which they applied for relief. Because nonresidents were generally ineligible for relief from existing public agencies, special provision for their care was included in the Federal Emergency Relief Act of May, 1933. In the administration of relief under this provision, transients were defined as unattached persons or family groups that had not resided for one continuous year or longer within the boundaries of the State at the time of application for relief.

Prior to the enactment of the Federal Emergency Relief Act of 1933, the number of transients was variously estimated to be between one and one-half and five million persons. These estimates proved to be greatly in excess of the number of transients who received care in accordance with the provisions of the Emergency Relief Act. A careful examination of registrations indicates that the maximum size of the transient relief population during the operation of the Transient Relief Program was 200,000 unattached persons and 50,000 family groups. But because the transient relief population was constantly undergoing a change of membership, it seems probable that the number of individuals and family groups that *at some time* received assistance from transient bureaus was two to three times these estimates.

The personal and occupational characteristics of this mobile relief population were determined from a study of monthly registrations in thirteen cities, selected to represent the several sections of the country. The more important findings of the study of characteristics may be summarized as follows:

(a) Approximately two-thirds of the unattached persons and one-half of the heads of family groups were between the ages of sixteen and thirty-five years.

(b) The proportion of unattached women did not exceed 3 percent in any month, while approximately 15 percent of the heads of family groups were women.

(c) The great majority of transients were native white persons; Negroes represented approximately one-tenth of the monthly registrations, and foreign-born whites, approximately one-twentieth. In the transient relief population the proportion of native white persons was higher, the proportion of foreign-born whites, lower, and the proportion of Negroes, about the same, as in the general population.

(d) Only 2 percent of the unattached transients and 3 percent of the heads of transient families had no formal education; approximately two-thirds of both groups had a grade-school education, or better.

1

(e) Ability and expressed willingness to work were reported for about 95 percent of the unattached persons and 90 percent of the heads of family groups.

(f) Broad groupings of usual occupations show that the proportion of unskilled and semi-skilled workers in the transient relief population was higher than the proportion of such workers in the general, or in the resident relief, population.

(g) The most frequent reason for the depression migration of needy persons and family groups was unemployment. Other reasons of importance were ill health, search for adventure, domestic trouble, and inadequate relief.

(h) When the origins of the transient relief population (total United States) are considered, it is found that unattached transients came principally from States to the east, and transient families from States to the west, of the Mississippi River.

(i) Based upon registrations in thirteen cities, approximately 80 percent of the unattached persons and 70 percent of the family groups came from urban centers (2,500 or more population). Moreover, transients from rural areas came more frequently from small towns (under 2,500 population) than from farms and open country.

(j) The largest and most persistent net gains in population resulting from the movement of transients were reported by States located in the Western and Southwestern sections of the country; while the largest and most persistent net losses were reported by States in the Eastern, Southeastern, and West Central sections.

The evidence presented in this report points to the conclusion that transiency was largely the result of two circumstances—widespread unemployment, and population mobility. The relief problem presented by this group was the result of a third factor—legal settlement (or residence) as a prerequisite for relief from public and private agencies in each community.

Except for the fact that they were non-residents, there seems little reason for considering transients as a distinct and separate group in the total relief population. Although they could be distinguished from the resident unemployed, it was principally because they were younger, and included a greater proportion of unattached persons. Actually the transient population represented the more active and restless element among the great number of unemployed created by the depression. Migration offered an escape from inactivity; and, in addition, there was the possibility that all communities were not equally affected by unemployment.

The migration of a considerable part of the transient relief population appears to have been a waste of effort. Much of the movement was away from urban areas that from the point of

view of economic development were more likely to afford employment than were the areas which particularly attracted the transient.   As business and industry recover, it may be expected
that many of the depression transients will return to areas
similar to the ones they left.

It seems evident from this study that the problem of depression transiency can be solved only through an adjustment
of this mobile labor supply to areas where there is a demand
for their services. Resettlement and stability are contingent
upon economic opportunity. Therefore, it seems highly probable
that the dissolution of the transient population will proceed
only as rapidly as business and industry can provide the employment essential to stability. To whatever extent this provision falls short, the transient problem will remain unsolved.

INTRODUCTION

The removal of individuals and family groups from one community to another is ordinarily the cause of no great concern to the communities affected. As long as those who move are self-supporting, and do not disturb the traditions, nor arouse the prejudices of the communities in which they stop, they are welcome. But when, as in 1930 and subsequent years, the movement of population includes an increasing number of unemployed persons in need of assistance, communities become alarmed, and either adopt the policy of "passing on" the needy to other communities, or refuse assistance on the grounds that their own residents have a prior claim on the public and private funds available for relief.

Either procedure is in keeping with the tradition in this country that each locality is responsible only for the care of its own needy citizens. The tradition is written into the statutes of most of the States, and has governed the poor relief practices in all of them. The doctrine of local responsibility for relief has a long history reaching back to English poor relief practices in the sixteenth century, when its avowed intent was to protect each parish from the inroads of "stalwart rogues" and "sturdy beggars". But neither in England where it originated, nor in this country where it was adopted, has the principle of local responsibility prevented the needy unemployed from quitting a community in which they could find no work. Moreover, poor relief procedure based upon this principle makes no attempt to distinguish the temporarily unemployed who have set out to find work, from the chronic wanderer—the hobo, the tramp, and the bum. By excluding all needy non-residents, the poor laws force the former to adopt the means of livelihood employed by the latter, with the result that some of the temporarily unemployed never resume a sedentary life.

The size of this mobile population has never been known, either in times of depression or prosperity. Social service agencies have long been familiar with the homeless man, the migratory worker, the runaway boy, the stranded workman, and other types of non-resident needy. These agencies knew that the number increased during depressions and declined during periods of prosperity. But with a population that was constantly moving, and largely anonymous, it was obviously impossible to estimate the total from the observations in any one agency, community or State.

For many years one or more of the social agencies in each of the large cities have been particularly concerned with the care of transient and homeless persons. These agencies gave what relief their funds permitted, arranged for the return of non-residents when the home community or relatives would accept

responsibility,   established means by which cases could be in-
vestigated with a minimum of delay,   and attempted to prevent
the needy non-resident from becoming a permanent social outcast.
But for every case that was helped,   there were many more that
either escaped notice   or could not be assisted.   The problem
was principally one of interstate migrations; and nothing short
of a change in the prevailing principle of local responsibility,
or Federal intervention,   could prevent a serious problem of
destitution with each recurring period of unemployment.

     Contrary to expectation, it was Federal intervention, rather
than a break with the tradition of local responsibility, that,
in 1933, made funds available for the relief of the needy non-
resident.   When the Seventy-third Congress met in the spring
of 1933, unemployment relief was recognized as a national problem.   The inability of the localities to care for the needs of
their citizens was frankly admitted; and the Federal Emergency
Relief Act of May, 1933,   provided for the cooperation of the
Federal Government with the States and communities in the relief
of destitution.   But this Act,   which by title and intent was
an emergency measure to assist the States, went even further;
it provided additional,   and wholly Federal funds for the care
of needy non-residents, or transients, who otherwise would have
remained an excluded group.

     The Relief Act of May, 1933, recognized that during an emer-
gency caused by nation-wide unemployment, the transient relief
population was necessarily a Federal responsibility. Thus, for
the first time it became not only possible, but necessary to
study the characteristics of a depression migration of needy
unemployed, and to determine the extent to which it represented
the chronic wanderer, and the sedentary person turned migrant
in search of a more favorable environment.

     It is the purpose of this report to present the results of
a study of the individuals and family groups who comprised the
transient relief population under the provisions of the Federal
Emergency Relief Act of May, 1933.

     The report consists of several sections, the first of which
defines the group and states the problem of the transient unemployed, reviews the efforts that were made to obtain consideration for them as a relief group,   and presents data on the
number of persons included.   The second section is concerned
with the personal characteristics of the two types of transient
relief cases—the individual case, or unattached transient,
and the group case, or transient family group. The next section
describes the occupational characteristics of unattached transients and heads of transient family groups, and discusses some
of the factors which condition their prospects of absorption
by private employment.   The fourth section is devoted to an

analysis of the reasons for the depression migration of individuals and family groups, the duration of their migration,
their origins in terms of the State of residence before migration, and their destinations in terms of States that gained
population as a result of this migration. The final section
summarizes the principal findings of this report, and discusses
the relation of the transient relief population to the general
problem of unemployment relief during the depression.

Chapter I

THE ORIGIN OF THE TRANSIENT RELIEF PROGRAM

During an economic depression the needy unemployed appear
as two distinct groups—the resident, and the non-resident
needy. The resident unemployed comprise much the larger group,
but they are known to the communities and accepted as a local
problem. The non-resident, or transient, unemployed, on the
contrary, are unknown, and readily become a source of alarm to
communities through which they pass. Although it now seems
evident that the alarm of the communities tends to exaggerate
the problem of the non-resident unemployed out of proportion
to the number on the road, the problem is no less real for
being overstated upon discovery.

Simply stated, the problem of the transient unemployed is
this: No community welcomes the needy stranger who comes either
as a competitor for what employment still remains, or as an
applicant for assistance, when both employment and relief funds
are inadequate to the needs of the resident population. In
effect, a depression puts a premium on length of residence and
stability; and those who venture to leave their home communities
in search of work must do so at the risk of being regarded with
suspicion, if not outright hostility. But to some of the unemployed, stability and enforced idleness are incompatible
states. Migration at least offers an escape from inactivity,
and in addition, there is the possibility that all communities
are not equally affected by unemployment.

Since a narrowing of the labor market is one of the first
signs of a depression, a migration of the unemployed might be
expected as an immediate consequence. What data are available
show this to have been the case in the most recent depression.
In October 1930 a report on social statistics, including the
number of transient and homeless persons receiving temporary
shelter in nineteen cities, contained the following statement:

> "Considering the seasonal influence on the
> (transient and homeless) service, it is interest-
> ing to note that in the more severe months of
> the first yearly quarter (1930), 8,533 more per-
> sons received aid this year than last in these
> 19 cities, whereas in the second quarter, 11,572
> more persons were assisted in 1930 than in 1929,
> in spite of the milder weather conditions." [1]

When reports from twenty-nine metropolitan areas were complete

---

[1] See Glenn Steele, Social Statistics, Monthly Labor Review, Vol. 31, Number 4, October, 1930.

for the year 1930, it was found that not only had the number
of nights' lodgings given transient and homeless men increased
in each quarter over comparable figures in 1929, but that in
the last quarter of 1930 the increase exceeded 100 percent.[1]
In 1931, a survey was made of the experience of sixteen cities
with the care of transient and homeless persons during the
winter of 1930-1931.[2] All but one of these cities reported a
marked increase in applications for relief over the previous
years.

Apparently the number of transient unemployed increased
steadily during the first half of 1931, and by fall some of the
communities became seriously alarmed. As it became evident
that conditions were not likely to improve during the winter
of 1931-1932, and that local resources were insufficient to
care for the resident unemployed, communities appealed for outside assistance in handling the needy transients. In November
1931, California authorized the establishment of labor camps
"where transient homeless men would be given food and shelter
in return for work on projects beneficial to the State of
California".[3] At about the same time a camp for non-resident
needy was established near Jacksonville, Florida. In December
1931, the Seventy-second Congress had under consideration two
unemployment relief bills, both of which included some provision for the non-resident unemployed. The provisions in these
bills were vague, reflecting the lack of knowledge as to the

---

[1] The agencies reporting were municipal lodging houses, missions, shelters,
religious, and other organizations that provided temporary shelter to transient and homeless men.
See Glenn Steele, Temporary Shelter for Homeless or Transient Persons,
United States Children's Bureau, Government Printing Office, Washington,
D. C., 1932.
[2] See Robert S. Wilson, Community Planning for Homeless Men and Boys, Family
Welfare Association of America, New York, 1931. See also Alderson and Rich,
Care of the Homeless in Unemployment Emergencies, published by the same
organization.
[3] See S. Rexford Black, Report on the California State Labor Camp, California
State Unemployment Commission, San Francisco, California, 1932, page 9.
The introduction to the report contains the following significant paragraphs:
"In the fall of 1931 the problem of caring for the unemployed homeless men
assumed serious proportions. The private relief agencies and the municipal
and county authorities found themselves confronted with the unexpected
problem of making provision for the increasing numbers of non-resident job-
less men who were pouring into our State in search of food and shelter,
and of the protection afforded by our favored climate."

"The mounting burden of unemployment was making deep inroads into the
limited funds that were available for relief to the resident unemployed,
and it became necessary for the State government to take immediate action
to relieve the local communities of the added responsibility of caring for
the non-resident transients."

number and the needs of the non-resident unemployed; but both
provisions recognized the fact that non-residents were ineligible for relief under existing practices.

The first bill, introduced on December 9, 1931, provided in
Section 6 (6) that States desiring to receive benefits from
this Act shall submit plans which shall include:

> *"...provisions satisfactory to the (Federal*
> *unemployment relief) board for securing the*
> *benefit contemplated by this act to persons*
> *within the State, irrespective of the period*
> *of residence within the State."*[1]

The second bill, introduced on the same date, provided in
Section 4 (5) that:

> *"The (Federal relief) board is authorized,*
> *through such means and agencies as it may*
> *determine, to provide for extending relief*
> *to migratory workers and their families,*
> *who by reason of inability to establish*
> *legal residence within any State, are un-*
> *·able to qualify for benefits under any State*
> *relief plan."*[2]

Although neither of these bills was specific on the subject
of relief to transients, some of the testimony introduced at
the public hearings held by the Senate committee referred directly to the problem, and indicated the growing concern in all
parts of the country.   One witness[3] when questioned about the
needs of the migratory worker, replied:

> *"You perhaps have noticed in the papers the*
> *news item that Florida was flashing warn-*
> *ings that it could not receive the hordes*
> *of people with very little or no money who*
> *were coming there to live. The same is*
> *true as to Georgia, California, Arizona,*
> *New Mexico, and many other States. The*
> *situation is complicated in those Western*
> *States by the fact that so many people go*

---

[1] S. 174, Seventy-second Congress, first session. For further information,
see Appendix A.
[2] S. 262, Seventy-second Congress, first session. See Appendix A.
[3] J. Prentice Murphy, Executive Director, Philadelphia Children's Bureau.
Hearings on S. 174 and S. 262, p. 51. See Appendix A.

> *west not only because they are poor or*
> *unemployed, but because they are sick or*
> *nearly so. They think that health lies at*
> *the other end of the line. Clearly a na-*
> *tional problem and a growing one. The*
> *actual number of unsettled migrants in terms*
> *of families and individuals may run up as*
> *high as 2,000,000."*

Another witness submitted a report on conditions in the several
States which showed that in some, transient relief was considered a more pressing problem than resident relief.[1]

Between the time when these first attempts were made to secure Federal assistance for the transient unemployed, and the
spring of 1933, several other efforts were made to obtain funds
for transient relief.[2] But it was not until the passage of the
Federal Emergency Relief Act of May, 1933, that these efforts
and the growing concern of the country over the problem resulted
in the provision of Federal funds for a transient relief program. Section 4(c) of the Federal Emergency Relief Act of May,
1933, provided:

> *"That the Administrator may certify out of*
> *the funds made available by this subsection*
> *additional grants to States applying there-*
> *for to aid needy persons who have no legal*
> *settlement in any one State or community." [3]*

---

[1] Frank Bane, Director, American Association of Public Welfare Officials,
Hearings on S. 174 and S. 262, pp. 106-107. See Appendix A. The following extracts are from Mr. Bane's report:
*"Arizona. The transient problem is most serious. Over half the relief
budgets are used for relief of transients. Phoenix reports a maximum of
1,780 transient men in one day.*
*"California. The indigent transient problem is most serious. Young men
are coming in large numbers, traveling on freight trains. It has been said
that Los Angeles already has over 70,000 transient men, with about 1,500
coming in daily. These Southwestern States are feeling the need for some
type of Federal aid for transients.*
*"Florida. Miami, Tampa, and Jacksonville are swamped by transients. The
sparsely settled counties are not aware of any special relief problems.
The State needs outside aid for the transient situation.*
*"Nevada. Local conditions are not especially serious, although the tran-
sient problem is becoming more acute.*
*"New Mexico. The transient problem causes most difficulty. One town of
2,000 reported a transient load of 2,000 during one month and others are
also carrying large transient loads."*
[2] From December 2, 1929, until March 4, 1933, there were 99 relief bills
introduced into Congress; twelve of these bills contained some provision
for relief to needy non-residents; and one of them (S. 5121) was solely
for transient relief. So far as can be determined, S. 174 and S. 262
referred to above, represent the first attempt during the depression to
obtain relief for transients. For further details on these twelve bills,
and the public hearings that were held on six of them, see Appendix A.
[3] Public—No. 15—73rd Congress, approved May 12, 1933.

LOCATION OF STUDY CITIES

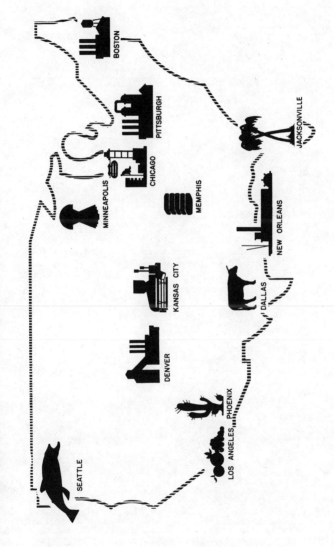

SEATTLE

MINNEAPOLIS

CHICAGO

PITTSBURGH

BOSTON

DENVER

KANSAS CITY

MEMPHIS

JACKSONVILLE

PHOENIX

DALLAS

NEW ORLEANS

LOS ANGELES

DIVISION OF SOCIAL RESEARCH   AF-1504

In accordance with this provision, a Division of Transient Activities was established as a part of the Federal Emergency Relief Administration. The States were invited to submit transient relief programs to be financed by relief grants ear-marked for that purpose; and by the close of 1933 there were in operation 261 transient relief centers and 63 work camps in 40 States.[1] Early in 1934 seven of the remaining States had programs approved, leaving only Vermont without a transient relief service.

The persons eligible for relief under this program were, according to the Relief Act of 1933, "...persons who have no legal settlement in any one State or community". Since the Act did not define what was meant by legal settlement, the reference was presumably to the legal settlement requirements of the several States. However, it was obviously impossible in practice to take account of the widely varying settlement provisions of the States[2] in providing relief to the interstate homeless. Therefore, resort was had to an arbitrary, but workable, definition of settlement, which was issued on July 11, 1933, in the Federal Emergency Relief Administration's "Rules and Regulations No. 3." Here it was stated that:

> *"For the purpose of this Act, settlement shall be defined as residence within a State for a period of ONE CONTINUOUS YEAR OR LONGER. Hence, all persons in need of relief who have not resided within the boundaries of a State for 12 consecutive months, may be considered as proper claims on the Federal Emergency Relief Administration under the above Section."*

In applying this definition of transient, it was realized that the homeless population would be divided into several classifications. These classifications were described in a memorandum issued July 26, 1933, by the Federal Emergency Relief Administration, on relief to transients and homeless:

> *"It should be remembered that in any local community there will be three types*

---

[1] For a description of the types of aid and the administration of relief under the Transient Relief Program see W. J. Plunkert, Public Responsibility of Transients, The Social Service Review, Vol. VIII, No. 3 (September, 1934) pp. 484-491.
[2] See Legal Research Bulletins Nos. A-1 to A-12, September 8, 1934, to February 15, 1935, Division of Research, Statistics, and Finance, Federal Emergency Relief Administration, Washington, D. C.
See also, Statutory Provisions for Financing Specific Categories of Welfare, prepared in August, 1935, by the same organization.

> *of homeless persons or families:*
> 1. *Local homeless residents*
> 2. *State homeless, more than twelve months in State*
> 3. *Transient homeless, less than twelve months in State.*
> *"All these groups need to be properly and humanely provided for. The groups (1) and (2) are provided for under Section 4(a) and 4(b) of the Federal Emergency Relief Act. Group No. 3 is provided for out of additional grants under Section 4(c) of the same Act."*

Thus, the homeless needy, which included persons of every degree of mobility from the chronic tramp to the recently evicted resident, were classified according to the length of time they had been in the State in which they applied for relief. This three-fold division was to have an important bearing on the size of the transient population.

The Size of the Transient Population — Estimated

Prior to the inauguration of the Transient Relief Program in July 1933, little was actually known of the number of needy homeless, resident or transient, despite the widespread concern over this group. However, there was no lack of estimates, particularly at Congressional hearings on relief legislation.[1] These estimates placed the number of needy homeless at one and one-half to five million persons. The Transient Relief Program had been in operation only a short time when it was discovered that these estimates greatly overstated the size of the transient homeless population as it was defined under the provision contained in the Relief Act of 1933. Judging from the number of transients who received care under the Transient Program, the number never exceeded one-half million. The overestimates of the transient population were largely the result of three factors: (1) the application of the term "transient"[2] to homeless

---

[1] Testimony of Dr. Nels Anderson, Columbia University, New York City, pp. 65-67, and J. Prentice Murphy, Philadelphia, page 84, at the hearings on S. 5121; and Mr. Murphy's testimony on S. 174 and S. 262, page 51. See Appendix A.

[2] In the field of relief the term "transient" came to have a somewhat more limited meaning after the passage of the Relief Act of 1933 than it had in the early years of the depression. During the Congressional hearings on relief legislation it was used more or less synonymously with the terms "homeless", "migrant", and "non-resident" to describe persons who were ineligible for relief under the provisions of State Poor Laws. During the operation of the Federal Emergency Relief Administration the word "transient" was applied specifically to needy persons and families that had been within a State less than twelve consecutive months at the time they applied for assistance. Not all of these persons were "transient" in the sense that they never remained long in one place; but there was a sufficiently large proportion of highly mobile persons included to justify acceptance of the word "transient" as a decided improvement on the ambiguous terms "homeless" and "non-resident".

persons or families without reference to whether or not they
had legal settlement in the community in which they applied
for assistance; (2) the estimation of the total population
from observation in areas where the number of transients was
causing the greatest alarm; and (3) the tendency of agencies
and individuals interested in obtaining assistance for transients to exaggerate the number on the road.

(1) The Federal Emergency Relief Administration's memorandum
of July 26, 1933, was the first attempt to segregate the homeless into local (resident), State (intrastate), and transient
(interstate) homeless. The public and private agencies —municipal lodging houses, missions, shelters, etc.—that had given
the needy homeless temporary shelter in the past, usually were
not concerned with the legal settlement status of the homeless
at time of application for relief. Indeed, at one time most of
these agencies did not even record the applicant's name, but
merely kept a record of the number of lodgings and meals given.
Although this practice of considering the homeless as anonymous
has gradually been replaced by a central record bureau or social
service exchange, the prevailing belief was that the transient
and homeless were practically identical; which, in fact, they
were, as far as local relief practices were concerned. It was
obvious that the transient was homeless, and experience had
shown that many of the homeless were transients.[1] Nels Anderson
stated at a Senate hearing[2] on transient relief legislation
that the only distinction between the transient and homeless
man was "the distinction that one is going."

The homeless were well known in every large city as a social
problem that varied in magnitude with economic conditions and
with the seasons.   They were to be found on the streets and
in the subways, the municipal lodging houses, the missions, the
Salvation Army soup kitchens, and in the "shanty towns"; weather
permitting, they could be seen along the docks and in the parks.
Certain sections of the large cities were well known as their
habitat; for instance, the Bowery in New York City, West Madison
and South State Streets in Chicago, and the "skid road" in
Seattle. The number of homeless was known to increase during
depressions, particularly during the winter months, over-crowd-
ing the poor facilities of the "flop houses" and the private
social agencies.   During the spring and summer, part of the
homeless population of the cities drifted out into the country
to work at short-time seasonal employments in agriculture,

---

[1] See Nels Anderson, The Hobo, Chicago, 1923, and The Homeless in New York
City (mimeographed), Welfare Council of New York City, 1934;   Alice W.
Solinberger, One Thousand Homeless Men, New York, 1911.
[2] Hearings on S. 5121, p. 66, January, 1933. See Appendix A.

construction, and such other industries as depend wholly or in part upon a floating labor supply. Each fall most of the wanderers returned to the cities, to live through the winter in cheap hotels if they had accumulated a "stake" or in the missions and free lodging houses if they had found no work or had spent their earnings.

It is not surprising, then, that in advance of the specific definition of transient issued by the Relief Administration, the estimates of the transient-homeless population should include, without discrimination, the resident and the migratory homeless. There is little doubt that the homeless in the cities did number a million or more; but there is no evidence to show that the migratory homeless ever reached such a figure. Moreover, the most reliable estimates[1] of the number of homeless in need of relief were based upon reports from the larger cities where there was no established procedure for differentiating transients, as later defined, from the resident (State or local) homeless.

(2) It was noted earlier in this chapter that the States which first became alarmed over the number of transients were California, Florida, Arizona, and New Mexico. There is no doubt that these States, because of their climate (which had been so extensively advertised) and location, exercised a particular attraction on the transient. Travel in these States frequently involves crossing sparsely settled areas where the traveler is immediately conspicuous, particularly if, like the transient, he rides the freight trains or hitch-hikes along the highways. Moreover, the cities in these States lacked the experience with the needy homeless that such cities as Seattle, Chicago, and New York had gained over a period of many years. Two thousand transients in Chicago, or New York City, might easily pass unnoticed, but the same number in Jacksonville, Florida; Lordsburg, New Mexico; Bakersfield, California; or Phoenix, Arizona, becomes a serious problem.

The Southern transcontinental route was favored by many of the transients traveling to and from the Pacific coast; and particularly by the younger transients who wanted to see the legendary Southwest. The railroad police and train crews were unable to prevent transients from riding freight trains through these sparsely settled areas; but the distance between cities made food and shelter hard to obtain. The result was that each through freight train brought its load of hungry men and boys who descended on the small town along the railroad seeking food and shelter.   The local police were helpless, for if no other

---

[1] See the results of the surveys conducted by the Committee on Care of Transient and Homeless, p. 20.

shelter was available, the transient sought out the jail, and,
if necessary, invited arrest to obtain assistance, safe in the
knowledge that he would not be detained any length of time.
When all else failed, the transient could generally find a
"jungle" on the outskirts of the town along the railroad right-
of-way inhabited by a group of his fellow travelers, where
questionable food and doubtful shelter might be obtained.

Under such circumstances it is not surprising that rumors
and reports were current that an "army of boys" was riding up
and down the length and breadth of the country, desperate and
anti-social, living to themselves along the tracks, begging
and stealing food and money, corrupted by the older tramps
and hoboes, a threat to morals, peace, and property; in short,
just such a group as has been described with lurid details in
the Sunday supplements as the "wild boys (and girls) of Russia".

These rumors and reports were not without some basis in
fact. Railroad employees confirmed the report of unprecedented
travel on the freight trains of transcontinental lines. The
Chief Special Agent of one of the railroads in the Southwest
made the following report at a Senate hearing:

> "On the Missouri Pacific Railroad we have been
> trying to pay some attention to what we at
> one time called migratory labor; that is, the
> transient movement... We took official notice
> in 1928, of 13,745 transients, trespassers
> that we found on our trains and property.
> "In 1929 that figure was 13,875.   In 1930
> we took a record of 23,892.
> "In 1931 that volume jumped to 186,028.
> "In 1932 it receded a little bit to
> 149,773..."[1]

As a result of rumors that large numbers of transient boys
were roaming the country, the United States Children's Bureau
in the spring of 1932 made a brief survey of the situation.
Information was obtained both from correspondence with local
officials and from the first-hand reports of a representative
who visited points in the South and West.[2]   In the report[3] of

[1] Hearings on S. 5121, January, 1933, pp. 35-36. See Appendix A. How many
more rode the trains without "official notice" is a matter of conjecture,
but it is probable that, at least, they equalled the number observed. Of
course, there were many duplications, that is, men observed at two or more
points on the same trip, or on different trips within the year. But then
this was only one of the railroads that found its freight trains carrying
an unusual number of transients.
[2] See testimony of Professor A. W. McMillen, University of Chicago, Hearings
on S. 5121, pp. 40-50. See Appendix A.
[3] See Twentieth Annual Report of the Chief of the Children's Bureau, Government Printing Office. Washington, D. C., 1932, pp. 5-7.

this survey no attempt was made to estimate the total number of
men and boys on the road; but evidence was cited to show that
the situation was particularly acute in the Southwest:

> *"Along the route of the Southern Pacific*
> *(Railroad) many small towns in Texas, New*
> *Mexico, and Arizona reported the daily*
> *passing of about 200 men and boys during*
> *the winter and spring. The Santa Fe*
> *(Railroad) at Albuquerque averaged 75 a*
> *day. From September 1, 1931, to April 30,*
> *1932, the Southern Pacific, with 9,130 miles*
> *of track, recorded 416,915 trespassers*
> *ejected."*
>
> . . . .
>
> *"In Phoenix, Arizona, during the three and*
> *a half months ended April 4, 1932, the*
> *Volunteers of America report feeding and*
> *lodging 1,529 different boys under 21...*
> *Yuma, (Arizona) which is on the main Southern*
> *Pacific line, reported feeding approximately*
> *30,000 men and boys at its 'soup kitchen'*
> *from November 1 to March 15. At least one-*
> *fifth were reported as under 21."*
>
> . . . .
>
> *"Social workers, police, and railroad men,*
> *who are in constant touch with these tran-*
> *sient boys, assert their belief that the*
> *overwhelming majority of them would nor-*
> *mally be in school or at work; that they*
> *are 'on the road' because there is nothing*
> *else to do; that they are, on the whole, not*
> *of the habitual 'hobo' or criminal type."*

From these and similar observations, there seemed to be a
factual basis for estimating the number of transients in the
country as a whole at well over a million persons; and there
is little question that estimates were influenced by the belief
that conditions in the Southwest were typical of other sections
where the transient was less readily observed because of greater
population density. Although the transient problem was, and
continued to be, serious in the Southwest, the number of transients, both men and boys, who received relief from transient
shelters and camps in these areas, never approached the number
suggested by these observations.

(3) The emphasis on the number of boys on the road was a

compound of sentiment and propaganda. Transient boys were good newspaper "copy", and special articles, personal accounts, and dramatic stories appeared in many of the metropolitan papers. Little was written of the older transients and homeless, the bums, the hoboes, and the migratory workers, except to hold them up as the awful examples of what was in store for this "army of youth".   Private agencies that for years had given some form of assistance to the homeless—transient and resident—saw in this growing concern for one part of the homeless population support for their argument that assistance was needed for the entire group; they knew that public opinion and legislative support would be more readily influenced by the dramatic aspects of youth on the march than by the drab and prosaic accounts of the hopeless disintegration of old men.

For many years these agencies, with but indifferent support from the public, had been the only source of assistance for the homeless person, young or old, resident or transient.   At a time when relief was foremost in the public mind, when demands were being made for Federal assistance for the resident unemployed, these agencies, firm in their insistence that the homeless needy must not continue to be a neglected group, and armed with years of experience, presented their case in its most compelling aspect.

It should be evident from this discussion of what seem to be the principal factors accounting for the over-estimates of the transient population, that there was a real need for information from the country at large, concerning the number requiring assistance. This need was recognized by the Committee on Care of Transient and Homeless (a private organization of prominent social workers) which undertook two surveys under the direction of Dr. Nels Anderson—the first in January, and the second in March of 1933.   It was the preliminary results of the first survey which were used by Dr. Anderson in estimating the size of the transient-homeless population at one and one-half million in his testimony at one of the Senate hearings[1] on transient relief. The second survey, made in March, 1933, to check the January returns, resulted in an estimate of one to one and one-quarter million persons.[2]

These two surveys provided the most conservative estimates

---

[1] See Hearings on S. 5121, January, 1933, p. 65. Dr. Anderson took care to point out that the results were tentative, and that they were secured with considerable difficulty and without adequate opportunity to check the accuracy of the returns.
[2] See Ellery F. Reed, Federal Transient Program, an Evaluative Survey, The Committee on Care of Transient and Homeless, pp. 19-20, New York, 1934. See also, Nels Anderson, Half a Million Old Men Without Homes, Social Security, December, 1933; and Gertrude Springer, Step Children of Relief, The Survey, June, 1933.

of the transient-homeless population; and, coming when they did,
undoubtedly played a part in obtaining special provision "....
to aid needy persons who have no legal settlement...." in the
Relief Act of 1933, which was passed a few months later. Although the estimates from these surveys were made from actual
count in many cities, there was at the time no basis for differentiating transient from resident homeless. As a measure of the
size of the needy homeless population—transient and resident—
these surveys probably understated rather than overstated the
number. It is highly probable that a census confined to agencies caring for the homeless would seldom include all of the
homeless needy.[1] But, as was soon discovered, the estimates
from these surveys did not agree with the number of transient
homeless who were to receive relief under the Transient Relief
Program.

The Size of the Transient Population—Registrations for Relief

With no more information as to the number of transient unemployed than was to be found in the incomplete reports of the
private social agencies, the local relief committees, and the
two surveys of the Committee on Care of Transient and Homeless,
the Federal Emergency Relief Administration inaugurated the
Transient Relief Program in the summer of 1933. The records
of those first months of operation are so confused that they
are of little value. It was not until January 1934 that reporting procedures were sufficiently established to permit anything approaching an accurate account of the number in the transient relief group; and then, it was discovered that the number
of transients eligible for relief was far below the estimates
that had been made. At first it was believed that this was the
direct result of the reluctance of States to apply for funds
to aid the needy non-resident; and special efforts were made
to establish transient relief programs in each of the forty-
eight States and the District of Columbia. But even when all

---

[1]The common practice of municipal lodging houses and many of the private
agencies was to allow resident homeless only three nights of lodging a
month, and the non-resident only one; this probably excluded many of the
homeless group from both of these censuses. Dr. Anderson, in discussing
his estimates, made the interesting comment:
*"And what about the old bum — the fellow who constitutes sixty to seventy
per cent of the breadline population? These fellows rarely get counted.
They congregate in the large cities. Year after year they go the rounds
living by odd jobs, 'mooching' and hanging around the agencies or the
saloons. A large number of them manage to get by without contacting any
agencies or only such agencies as would not report in the case of an in-
ventory which we tried to conduct. There is no way I know of counting the
aged and derelict homeless of the great cities. It is my conviction they
far outnumber the mobile youth in our transient camps."*
From a memorandum to the writer, May 31, 1935.

but one of the States (Vermont) had programs in operation, the
number of transients remained far below the estimates of a
million or more.

Despite the steady improvement in reporting procedures de-
veloped by the Division of Transient Activities, it was never
possible to determine with any degree of accuracy the size of
the transient relief population.   Actually, the transient unemployed were not a definite and fixed group in the total relief population.   On the contrary, the transient unemployed
were a relief population that changed its membership constantly,
and was never the same on any two days in any one place. It
was a population that included some who crossed the continent
within a month; some whose movements were restricted to a ra-
dius of a hundred miles of the place they once called home; and
still others who drifted slowly from North to South, or East
to West, and back as the seasons, employment opportunities,
rumor, or curiosity directed.

The measurement and description of the transient relief
population was a decidedly different problem from that presented
by the larger resident relief group. The mobility of the former stood in contrast with the immobility of the latter.   The
two censuses of the Committee on Care of Transient and Homeless
(January and March, 1933), were evidence that even the apparently simple task of counting the transients was more complex
than had been realized. The Division of Transient Activities
was concerned with the administration of transient relief, and
its reports[1] were designed primarily to show the number and
type of transient relief cases. If transiency, as a depression
phenomenon, was to be studied, a special investigation was
needed.   Therefore, early in 1934, the Division of Research,

---

[1] The Division of Transient Activities issued the following reports in
mimeographed form:
   Census of Transients Under Care. A mid-monthly count by States and type
of case (i.e., unattached, family groups, interstate, intrastate, local
homeless), of the total number of persons receiving relief in centers and
camps during the 24-nour period of the 15th or 16th of the month.   The
first census was taken on February 15, 1934; but the first report issued
was that of the April 16 census. Summaries of these censuses, beginning
with that of February 15, 1934, are to be found in the Monthly Report of
the Federal Emergency Relief Administration, Government Printing Office,
Washington, D. C.
   Census Report on Age, Race and Sex, of All Individuals Under Care. A
quarterly census of all persons under care in centers and camps on the
last day of the quarter, consolidated for the United States. The first
census of this type was taken on September 30, 1934, and issued in final
form on March 4, 1935.
   Origin of Persons Receiving Relief at Each State Transient Division. A
quarterly census of all persons under care in centers and camps on the
last day of the quarter, by States, showing the State of origin. The first
census of this type was taken on September 30, 1934, and issued in March,
1935.

Statistics, and Finance of the Federal Emergency Relief Administration undertook, in the form of a special study, the task of
providing detailed information about the transient relief population for the use of the Relief Administration and for such
other individuals and organizations as were interested in this
particular relief problem. This study, made by the Research
Section, was based upon transient relief registrations in thirteen cities which were selected on a basis of their importance
as transient centers and their representativeness of the several
sections of the United States. [1]

For more than a year, May 1934 through June 1935, the
Research Section collected, tabulated, and analyzed data drawn
from the registrations of transients in these cities. At the
time the study was started a choice had to be made between two
methods of collecting information: (1) a periodic census of all
those under care on one full day; and (2) a continuous account
of all who registered day by day and month by month. The census method, when applied to the transient population, may be
likened to the periodic closing of the entrances and exits of
a large railway station for the purpose of counting those just
come and those about to go; while the method of continuous registrations may be likened to the gate keeper's daily record of
all those who come and go. It should be apparent that neither
method provides an exact account of those in transit; but it
should also be apparent that the two methods set an upper and
lower limit to the population in any one month. The census
method understates the population because it cannot include
those en route; while the registration method overstates the
population by reporting the more mobile individuals at two or
more points within the same registration period. Although it
was not known that these two methods would yield strikingly
different results when applied to the transient relief population, it was decided to base the Research Section's study on
continuous registrations, summarized monthly. [2]

In its monthly reports of total registrations and cases under
care, the Division of Transient Activities employed both the
registration and the census method of collecting data. [3] The
striking difference in the results obtained can be seen in

[1] The cities were: Boston, Chicago, Dallas, Denver, Jacksonville (Fla.),
Kansas City (Mo.), Los Angeles, Memphis, Minneapolis, New Orleans, Phoenix,
Pittsburgh, and Seattle.
[2] For the monthly summaries and other reports from this study, see Research
Bulletins Nos. B-26, B-32, B-55, C-12, C-18, D-7, TR-1, TR-2, TR-3, TR-4,
TR-5, TR-6, TR-7, TR-8, TR-9, Research Section, Federal Emergency Relief
Administration, Washington, D. C.
[3] Because of the practice of the Division of Transient Activities of issuing
monthly the results obtained by the census method, the equally significant
registration data have frequently been overlooked.

Chart I, which represents total registrations of unattached transients and the number under care in the United States for the fifteen-month period January 1934 through April 1935. The solid line represents continuous registrations by months, and the broken line the number under care on the 15th of each month, February 1934 through April 1935. The data from which this chart was made are to be found in Table 1, Appendix B.

The one-day, mid-monthly census of unattached transients (i.e., the unaccompanied individual) shows a fairly steady increase, February through December 1934, while total registrations mount sharply from February through August and then decline irregularly until the marked increase of March 1935. Total registrations were strongly affected by seasonal influences, while the mid-monthly census was singularly free from these influences. In March of both 1934 and 1935, the registration of unattached transients turned upward with the return of moderate weather; and in 1934, the increase continued until September, when the approach of fall and winter weather reduced mobility and, consequently, registrations. The decline from the August peak continued irregularly throughout the winter months until the seasonal expansion of March 1935 reversed the trend.

In comparing registrations in March 1934 with those in March 1935, it is apparent that the seasonal increase in the latter year began at a higher level. This reflects both the growth in the number of unattached transients receiving relief during the year, and particularly the increase in facilities for their care. It does not necessarily mean that the number of unattached transients increased during this period; probably it means little more than that transients who formerly went without care or were forced to depend on over-night shelter in missions and jails came into the transient bureaus as facilities were expanded. [1]

This explanation is supported by reference to the number of unattached transients under care on the 15th of each month during the period under consideration. (See mid-monthly census,

---

[1] A rough idea of the expansion can be gained from the following figures:

	Centers	Camps	Camps under construction
February, 1934	249	85	--
March, 1935	283	284	28

It should be understood that a *center* can have many *shelters* and that there was a greater expansion of facilities for care than the small increase in *centers* would indicate.

Chart I.) From February 1934, when this census began, through December 1934 the number under care increased each month; thereafter a slight decline set in. During the twelve months, March 1934 to March 1935, the number under care as reported by the mid-monthly census increased by 92 percent, while registrations in March 1935 were 104 percent higher than in March of the previous year. This suggests that the mid-monthly census provides a fairly accurate description of the *trend* in transient relief activities, while the monthly registrations describe the *seasonal variation*.

Seasonal influences played a lesser part in registrations of transient family groups than was the case with unattached transients. On the other hand, the number of families under care rose more rapidly; and at all times during the period February 1934 through April 1935 the number under care reported by the mid-monthly census varied from almost twice to more than three times the number of registrations during the month. (See Chart II; and Table I, Appendix B.) From this it appears that the family groups came into the transient relief population at a lower rate, and tended to remain under care in one place a longer period of time, than did the unattached transients [1].

Registrations in the thirteen cities which served as the basis for the Research Section's special study of transients are shown in Chart III; and in Table I, Appendix B. There is apparent in these data a general agreement with the results for the country as a whole, shown in Charts I and II. A complete comparison for the fifteen-month period is not possible, since data for the thirteen cities are not available prior to May 1934. However, from May through August, registrations of unattached transients in the thirteen cities increased when registrations for the country as a whole were increasing, and turned downward at the same point. The decline, while more regular in the thirteen cities, was of approximately the same proportion as for the country as a whole, and terminated at the same point, February 1935. Registrations of transient family groups correspond only in part: there was the increase to a peak in August 1934, the low point in February 1935, and the absence of wide seasonal fluctuations.

The purpose of this brief discussion of registrations for the country as a whole is: (1) to fix an upper and lower limit to the size of the transient relief population; (2) to demonstrate the difference in returns obtained from reports of monthly registrations and from the mid-monthly census; and (3) to

---

[1] Proof of the lower mobility of transient family groups is presented in Chapter 4.

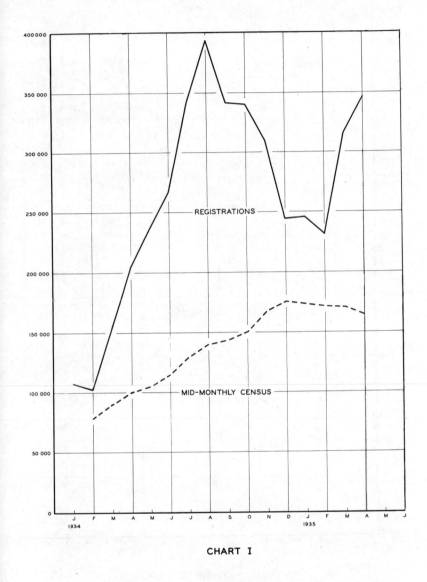

CHART I

REGISTRATIONS AND MID-MONTHLY CENSUS

UNATTACHED TRANSIENTS

UNITED STATES TOTAL

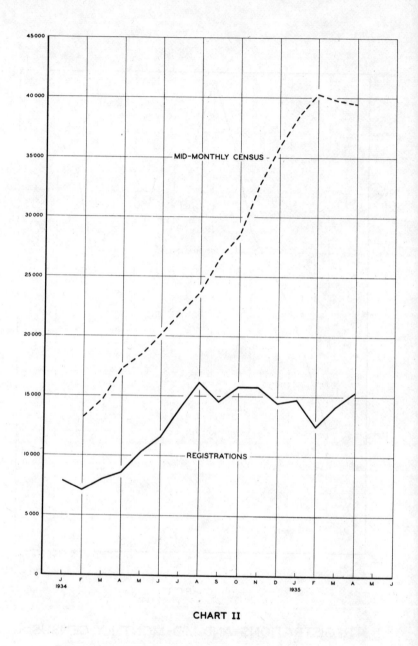

CHART II

REGISTRATIONS AND MID-MONTHLY CENSUS
TRANSIENT FAMILY GROUPS
UNITED STATES TOTAL

show that registrations in the thirteen cities included in the Research Section's study varied much as did registrations in the country as a whole.   Most of the findings of this report are conditioned by one or more of these factors.   Throughout the pages that follow, frequent reference will be made to "the transient relief population", although the number of persons included in that population can be determined only by approximation between limits that changed from month to month.   In the description of the personal characteristics of this population most of the data are taken from records of continuous registrations, although it is known that the distribution of some of these characteristics differed significantly when taken from the records of a one-day census. And finally, the greater part of the data used in describing the transient relief population was obtained from registrations in thirteen study cities, where purely local circumstances occasionally had a marked, though temporary, effect upon registrations.   In justification of the use of data from thirteen cities to describe the larger population, it is argued that a complete and detailed description of the total population was impossible; that the cities selected were well distributed geographically; and that total registrations in these cities not only varied much as did registrations in the country as a whole,   but represented from 7.1 to 8.3 percent of all unattached transients registered each month, and from 11.5 to 15.9 percent of all transient family groups.

Chapter II

THE PERSONAL CHARACTERISTICS OF THE
TRANSIENT RELIEF POPULATION

In view of the confusion that existed as to the number of
needy non-residents before the Transient Relief Program was
initiated, it is not surprising to find that nothing was known
of their personal characteristics. Using data obtained from
registrations in the thirteen study cities, this chapter will
be devoted to a description of the transient relief population
in terms of the conventional categories of social statistics.
Because it is believed that this information is important in
itself, the emphasis throughout this chapter will be upon statistical description. However, brief interpretations are included whenever the data permit. The reader who is interested
in only a general statement of personal characteristics is
referred to the final section of the report, where a brief
summary of this chapter is presented.

This chapter will be concerned with a description of the
age, sex, color or nativity, marital status, and education of
unattached transients and heads of family groups. For reasons
which will become apparent, the unaccompanied individual, or
to use the established terminology, the unattached transient,
will be treated separately from the responsible individual, or
"head", of a group traveling together. On the basis of registrations, unattached transients consistently represented more
than four-fifths of all persons—unattached, family heads,
and other members of family groups—included in the transient
relief population; but on the basis of the mid-monthly census
the proportion of unattached transients varied from three-fifths
to one-half of the total population. Since the transient group,
or "family", consisted on the average of three persons, only
one of whom, the "head", is considered in most of the descrip-
tions which follow, the preponderance of unattached transients
is accentuated.

Age

Among the personal characteristics of the transient relief
population, perhaps the most striking is age. During the
twelve-month period, May 1934 through April 1935, two-thirds
or more of the unattached transients registered in the thirteen
study cities were under thirty-five years of age, and the median age was consistently under thirty years. (See Table 2a,

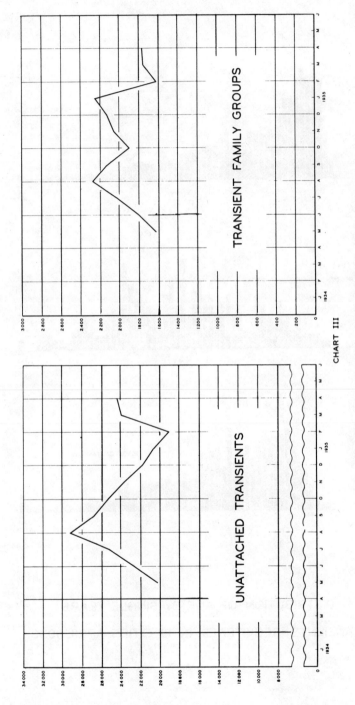

CHART III

TRANSIENT REGISTRATIONS—13 CITIES

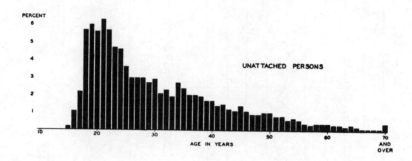

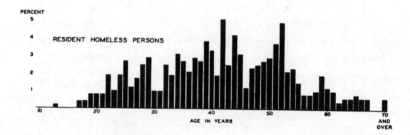

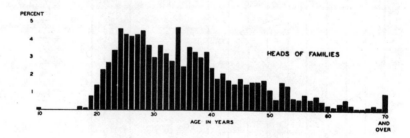

CHART IV

DISTRIBUTION OF AGE BY SINGLE YEARS,
TRANSIENTS REGISTERED IN 13 CITIES, APRIL, 1935.

Appendix B.) During the same period the percentage of unattached transients forty-five years of age or older varied from
a low of 12 percent to a high of 16 percent, indicating clearly
that transiency was the resort of the younger members among the
unemployed in the general population. But the evident youth of
the unattached was not a confirmation of the dire prediction
that an "army of boys" was on the road. In none of the twelve
months reported in Table 2a does the proportion of unattached
transients under twenty years of age exceed one-fifth of the
total. By far the majority of the unattached transients were
between the ages of twenty and forty-five years, with the greatest concentration between twenty and thirty-five years of age.
The youth of the unattached transient relief population is well
illustrated in Chart IV, which shows, by single years, the age
of unattached transients, resident homeless persons, and heads
of family groups registered in the thirteen study cities during
April 1935.

Both before and during the operation of the Transient Relief
Program, interest was centered on the youngest group in the
transient population—the boys and girls under twenty years of
age. It has been stated above that the number of juveniles on
the road was found to be less than had been predicted; nevert he-
less, they represented a social problem greater than their number indicated. The proportion of younger transients varied with
the seasons; increasing during the spring and summer months when
weather conditions were favorable to travel, and decreasing during the fall and winter months when inclement weather restricted
mobility.

Among the unattached transients registered for relief in the
thirteen study cities, the proportion under twenty years of age
rose from 15 percent in May 1934, to 20 percent in July and
August, and fell to 12 percent in December, 1934. In general,
the proportion of younger transients rose when registrations
were increasing, and fell when registrations were declining.
(See Chart III, for registrations.) However, the proportion of
transients under twenty years of age increased slightly in both
January and February, 1935, when the trend of registration in
the thirteen cities (and in the country as a whole) was downward, preceding by two months the expected seasonal rise in
registrations which occurred in March.

The seasonal variation in the proportion of younger transients
differed markedly in the several sections of the country. In
August 1934, when registrations were at a maximum, Boston reported that 4 percent of the unattached transients were under
twenty years of age, compared with 6 percent in February 1935,
when registrations were at a minimum. Evidently Boston (and

probably most of New England) did not attract the younger transients.   In contrast, Chicago reported that 7 percent of the
unattached were under twenty years of age in December 1934,
and in January 1935, when registrations were declining; and
21 percent in August 1934, when registrations were at a peak.
The highest proportions of younger transients were reported by
cities in the South and the Southwest.   One-quarter of the
unattached transients registered in Jacksonville, Florida, in
August 1934, were under twenty years of age; New Orleans reported 24 percent in August; and so did both Dallas and Los
Angeles in June and July, 1934. In each of these cities, total
registrations were lower during the summer than during the winter months, exactly the opposite of the situation in such cities
as Chicago, Denver, and Pittsburgh.   However, in twelve of the
thirteen cities studied, the proportion of transients under
twenty years of age was highest during the summer months.

The general conclusion to be drawn is that the younger transients came into the population during the summer months; and
this applies to areas where registrations were low during these
months as well as to areas where registrations were high.   The
increase in the proportion of younger transients occurred at the
same time that registrations were increasing in the country as
a whole, as well as in the thirteen cities as a group. But the
rise in registrations was only partly the result of the increase
in the number of younger transients. In absolute numbers there
was an increase in the number of transients in all age groups,
but the relative increase tended to be more pronounced among
the younger group.

In considering the reasons for the summer increase in the
registrations of the younger group, it seems probable that the
correspondence between the increase in registrations and the
occurrence of the school vacation period was more than a co-
incidence. This does not imply that all of the increase can be
explained by this circumstance, but only that recruits from the
school group during the vacation period were of considerable
importance. Careful interviewing of the younger transient frequently elicited the frank statement that he was on the road
less from economic necessity than from a desire to see the
country when favorable weather and facilities for his care made
transiency preferable to inactivity in his home community.
Moreover, there seems little question that during the depression
years, high school and college students found little of the
employment that once occupied them during the summer months.
Under the circumstances it is not surprising that, during the
vacation period, some of the more adventurous students from the
schools and colleges of the country should have been included

among the registered transients. In this connection it is significant that cities in the South and Southwest, which traditionally possessed a strong attraction for the younger group,
reported the highest proportion of transients under twenty years
of age during the summer months when total registrations in
these areas were low.   By their own report,   States that particularly appealed to the younger transient were Florida, Louisiana (particularly New Orleans), Texas, Arizona, New Mexico, and
California. Not to have visited these States seems to have been
considered a mark of the novice. In addition to those who expected to resume their schooling in the fall,   there were also
those whose formal education had ended with the close of the
school term and who therefore faced the necessity of self-support.
During a period of prolonged unemployment it might be expected
that the transient population would receive additions from this
annual increase in the labor supply.

The heads of family groups were, on the whole, somewhat older
than the unattached transients. (See Table 2b, Appendix B; and
Chart IV.) However, the difference was more the result of the
very small proportion of family heads under twenty years of age,
and, compared with the unattached, the smaller proportion twenty
to twenty-four years of age, than of any great increase in the
proportion of family heads advanced in years. This is evident
from a comparison of the proportions of each group forty-five
years of age and older.   Among the unattached the proportion
varied from 12 to 16 percent; while among the heads of family
groups the variation was from 18 to 22 percent.   Further comparison of the distributions in Tables 2a and 2b shows that
while the proportion of unattached transients twenty to twenty-
four years of age was consistently higher than in the case of
family heads, the reverse was true of the proportions twenty-five
to thirty-four, and thirty-five to forty-four years of age. The
greatest concentration of ages for the unattached was between
twenty and thirty-five years of age, with the median age between
twenty-five and thirty years; the greatest concentration of ages
for family heads was between twenty-five and forty-five years
of age, with the median age between thirty-three and thirty-five
years.   Therefore, as measured by the medians, the heads of
family groups were from five to eight years older than the unattached.

Although the heads of transient family groups were in general
somewhat older than the unattached, they were younger than either
the heads of resident relief families or those in the population
at large.   Here, as with the unattached transient, there is
evidence of a close relationship between youth and mobility; but,
in the case of family group heads, a mobility that was seriously

restricted by the presence of women and children, and by the difficulties of travel by a group without adequate resources.

It was suggested earlier in this report that transiency was a depression migration of unemployed persons and family groups. It may now be added that transiency was a depression migration of individuals and family groups from among the younger members of the great body of the unemployed. Family groups, even more than the unattached, are evidence of the social and economic pressure that created a mobile population of needy unemployed, since the transiency of family groups represented a much more definite break with home and community life than did the wanderings of unattached transients who frequently had a home to which they could return. It is highly probable that the completeness of the break with community life was an important factor in keeping the number of transient families considerably under the number of unattached transients. But this consideration should serve to stress the important social problem that is raised when family groups turn to transiency as the means of finding a place where they can again be self-supporting.

This discussion of age would be incomplete without some mention of the resident, or local, homeless persons who, until the operation of the Transient Relief Program demonstrated otherwise, were believed to be an integral part of the transient population. Though technically excluded from relief as transients because they had legal settlement, or the presumption of settlement, in the community, the resident homeless unattached were frequently cared for by the transient bureaus in accordance with an administrative arrangement which centralized the care of all unattached homeless persons. It was noted in Chapter 1 that the resident homeless unattached persons represented a social problem that was well known in the larger cities. In this chapter it will be possible to show that the transient and resident homeless differed as to personal characteristics, and particularly as to age.

The transient bureaus in only six of the thirteen cities included in the Research Section's study accepted resident homeless relief cases;[1] but from these six cities enough cases were reported to determine the age characteristics of this group. The age distribution of resident homeless registered for relief during the period October 1934 through April 1935, is shown in Table 2c, Appendix B; and for one month (April 1935) by single years, in Chart IV.

The resident homeless were a distinctly older group than

[1]The cities were: Denver, Jacksonville (Fla.), Los Angeles, Minneapolis, Pittsburgh, and Seattle.

the transient relief population. This can be shown most readily
by the difference in the proportion under twenty-five years and
over forty-four years of age, and by the median age, in comparison with these same measures taken from the age distributions
of unattached transients and of heads of transient family groups.
When this is done for the comparable period, October 1934
through April 1935, the results as derived from Tables 2a, b,
and c, Appendix B, are:

	PERCENT		YEARS
	UNDER 25 YEARS	OVER 44 YEARS	MEDIAN AGE
UNATTACHED TRANSIENTS	37 TO 42	12 TO 16	27 TO 30
HEADS OF FAMILY GROUPS	15 TO 17	18 TO 22	33 TO 35
RESIDENT HOMELESS UNATTACHED	6 TO 8	40 TO 49	42 TO 45

From this comparison it is evident that not only were the
resident homeless unattached distinctly older than the transient
unattached with whom they are most nearly comparable, but that
they were likewise older than the heads of family groups. Actually, the comparison with family heads is not valid since
resident homeless families were not given relief in transient
bureaus; but the comparison is interesting because it shows
that the resident homeless were older than either of the transient groups.

Lest it be objected that the data used were not representative because only a part of the homeless in these six cities
were included in the transient bureau registrations, and that,
therefore, the age characteristics obtained are not valid, cor-
roborating evidence as to the age of the resident homeless in
New York City may be offered from a study made by Dr. Nels
Anderson. In discussing the age distribution of 19,861 resident homeless men registered at the Central Registration Bureau, New York City, October 1931 to April 1932, Dr. Anderson
states:

> *"We note that 8.2 percent of the Central
> Registration Bureau homeless are under
> 25 years...In the middle-age groups the
> homeless bulk large...Thus, the homeless
> population in New York is largely middle-
> aged men, with a median age of about 41
> years..."*[1]

---

[1]Nels Anderson, The Homeless in New York City (mimeographed), Welfare Council of New York City, February, 1934, pp. 165-166.

Furthermore, Dr. Anderson points out that the median age of 14,194 homeless men enumerated by the 1930 Census in the Bowery area of New York City was forty-two years, and that the median age of homeless men at two of the Salvation Army's industrial plants were forty-one and forty-seven years, respectively. The remarkably close agreement between Dr. Anderson's findings for the homeless of New York City and the returns from six of the cities included in the Research Section's study of transients, seems to leave little doubt as to the age differential between the resident homeless and the transient groups.

Before closing this discussion of age characteristics, something should be said of the difference between age distributions obtained by the Research Division's study from continuous registrations in thirteen cities, and those obtained by the Division of Transient Activities from a one-day quarterly census. In the discussion of registration trends it was demonstrated that the two methods of obtaining data on the transient relief population—continuous registrations and a periodic census—provided returns that differed markedly. The difference may be demonstrated further by comparing age data derived from continuous registrations in thirteen cities with age data from a quarterly census for the country as a whole.

The age distribution of all unattached persons under care on March 31, 1935, as reported to the Division of Transient Activities, showed that. 23 percent were under twenty-five years of age; that 32 percent were over forty-five years; and that the median age was approximately thirty-six years. In contrast, the age distribution of unattached transients registered in the thirteen study cities during the month of March 1935, showed that 42 percent were under twenty-five years of age; that 12 percent were over forty-five years; and that the median age was between twenty-seven and twenty-eight years. Measured by the medians, the unattached were from eight to nine years older when the census method was used to determine age than when the method was that of continuous registrations. Similar contrasts were found for other quarterly census returns. A comparison of the age characteristics of family group heads is not possible since the Transient Division's quarterly census[1] does not distinguish heads from other members of family groups.

There are at least two known factors that assist in explaining this marked difference in age characteristics obtained from

---

[1] See footnote 1, page 19, Chapter 1, for a description of the Transient Division's quarterly census. Age was reported separately for all unattached persons and all family group persons, but the age of family group heads was not reported separately from the age of other members of the family group.

the registration and from the census method of collecting data.
The first, and most important, is the difference in mobility of
young and old. Most of the older transients had seen enough of
the country to satisfy their curiosity; and they knew how little
chance there was of a homeless man forty-five years of age, or
older, finding employment during the depression. As a result,
they tended to accumulate in transient bureaus and camps, where
they were counted at each census. On the other hand, the
younger transients—and particularly those under twenty-five
years of age—were impatient of transient bureaus and camps.
Curiosity led them into every part of the country; and for some
time at least after joining the transient population, they
honestly believed that employment could be found in some place
other than in their home community. As a result, they were by
far the most mobile group in the relief population; the few reports on length of stay in transient bureaus by age groups show
that the transients under twenty-five years of age stayed on the
average less than three days. From this it seems obvious that
the more mobile the person, the more time he spent outside of
transient bureaus, and, therefore, the greater the chance of
being missed by a one-day census at three-month intervals.

But it is also apparent that the more mobile individuals
would be included more than once in a continuous account of the
registrations for the country as a whole and for the thirteen
cities as a group, during any one month. Therefore, it seems
logical to conclude that age distributions derived from continuous registrations in the thirteen cities were weighted by the
younger and more mobile persons, while age distributions derived
from a one-day quarterly census were weighted by the older and
less mobile persons.

The second, and less important, factor making for the older
age of unattached transients as reported by the quarterly census is that the resident homeless, a distinctly older group,
were included by some of the centers where both resident and
transient homeless were given care by transient bureaus. While
efforts were made to avoid confusing the two groups, it is known
that such confusion did occur, with the result that the age
level of unattached transients was raised to some extent.

Sex

The more sensational accounts of the transient population
written prior to the inauguration of the Transient Relief Program
implied that the presence of women and girls on the road was a

social problem second only to that of the transient boy.[1] In the absence of any definite knowledge concerning the transient population, the exceptional case could be exploited and, by implication, exaggerated all out of proportion, without fear of contradiction. Thus the girl transient, from a few lurid and sensational accounts, assumed an importance in the public mind that the undramatic reports from transient bureaus have not entirely corrected. Among the inquiries about the transient that came to the Research Section and Transient Division, the question, "How many women are there on the road?" was almost as frequent as questions about the transient boy.

The answer is that, relatively, unattached women were a minor problem in the provision of relief to the transient unemployed. The proportion of unattached women included in the registrations in the thirteen cities studied by the Research Section are presented, by months, in Table 3, Appendix B. There it is seen that women constituted only about 2 percent of the total unattached transient population and that this proportion was fairly constant, month after month. Nor is the sex ratio materially altered when determined from the quarterly census[2] of all unattached persons under care as reported to the Division of Transient Activities. Out of approximately 170,000 unattached transients reported by the December 31, 1934, census and a like number by the census of March 31, 1935, only about 4,700 or 2.8 percent, were women. However, there is no intention in this account of minimizing the problem of unattached and homeless women transients by demonstrating their relatively minor proportion of the total. The very fact that unattached women were included among the unattached transients is ample indication of a serious personal and social problem that should not be minimized.

The explanation for the small proportion of unattached women transients is not hard to find. The wanderings of unattached women were beset with more difficulties than was the case with unattached men. Travel without resources, as practised by unattached transients, was largely a matter of riding freight and passenger trains illegally, and the solicitation of rides in automobiles and trucks. For the former means of travel women are less fit physically, and even success at the latter was not free from hazards. Moreover, women are novices at unattached wandering, and in addition are likely to encounter both

---

[1]For example, see Thomas Minehan, Boy and Girl Tramps of America, New York, 1934, particularly Chapter IX, Sex Life. See also Nels Anderson's criticism of the erroneous emphasis placed on boy and girl transients in this book, The Survey, January 1935, pp. 26-27.
[2]See footnote 1, page 19, Chapter 1.

suspicion and prejudice from citizen and police alike. For all of these reasons it would seem logical to expect—what the data confirm—that a relatively small proportion of unattached transients were women.

Among the heads of family groups, the proportion of women was much higher, even though, like the unattached, family group heads were predominantly male. During the twelve-month period under consideration, the proportion of women heads varied from 11.8 to 16.5 percent. Family groups traveled most frequently by automobile; and this circumstance, plus the protection to be derived from group travel, helps to explain the greater proportion of women as heads of transient family groups than as unattached transients.

Taking all members of family groups into account, it is seen from Table 3 that the proportion of females was slightly, but consistently, in excess of males. Although the majority of family groups were composed of husband and wife, or husband, wife, and one child, there were more families consisting of a woman only and children than of a man only and children. This probably accounts for the slight preponderence of females among all members of family groups.

Color and Nativity

Transiency was predominantly the migration of native white persons. During the nine-month period, August 1934 through April 1935, shown in Table 4, Appendix B, from 82 to 88 percent of the unattached, and from 84 to 91 percent of the heads of family groups registered in the thirteen cities were native white. The proportion of foreign-born whites among the unattached varied from 4 to 5 percent, and among the heads of family groups from 3 to 8 percent. The proportion of Negroes was consistently higher among the unattached than among the heads of family groups: From 7 to 12 percent of the unattached were Negroes, in comparison with from 4 to 6 percent of the heads of family groups. Mexicans, Orientals, and Indians were returned as other races; and these groups combined account for only 1 to 2 percent of the unattached, and 1 to 3 percent of the heads of family groups.

When the color and nativity characteristics of the transient population are compared with those of the general population (1930 Census), it is found that the proportion of native whites in the transient population was higher than their proportion in the general population. The foreign-born whites, on the other hand, were represented in the transient population in only about half their proportion in the general population;

while Negroes appeared in the transient population in a slightly smaller proportion than in the general population.[1]

The preponderance of native white transients suggests that they turned to transiency more readily than did members of the other color and nativity groups. In view of the long tradition of population mobility in this country, and the large-scale population movements revealed by the birth-residence data of the decennial censuses,[2] it is not surprising to find that the transient population was composed mainly of native white persons.

The small proportion of foreign-born white persons in the transient population would seem to indicate that transiency did not offer them a solution for their social and economic problems during the depression. In recent years the foreign born have tended to concentrate in the large industrial centers immediately upon their arrival in this country. This is evident from the 1930 Census, which shows that foreign-born whites represented about 16 percent of the urban population, about 5 percent of the rural population, and about 11 percent of the total population. It seems probable that the maintenance of racial or national ties in the urban centers, as well as the tendency to maintain close-knit family units, would act as a deterrent to transiency for the foreign born. In addition, social pressure, to some extent, immobilizes the foreign-born groups.

Traditionally, the Negro has been a relatively immobile group in the population; the only really striking example of shift in the Negro population in recent years was the movement of Negro workers from the South to the North during and following the World War, when employment opportunities became available as the result of the cessation of immigration and of the increasing use of unskilled and semi-skilled workers by large-scale industries. This migration of Negro workmen is, in all probability, one major reason for the disproportionately large number of Negroes on relief in the large industrial centers of the North.[3] Indeed, the proportion of Negroes on relief for the country as a whole was considerably larger than their proportion in the total population of 1930[4]. Despite this fact,

---

[1] See Fifteenth Census, Population, Vol. II, Table 10.
[2] See Thornwaite, Internal Migration in the United States, Philadelphia, 1934; and Galpin and Manny, Interstate Migrations among the Native White Population, U. S. Dept. of Agriculture, Washington, D. C., 1934.
[3] See The Unemployment Relief Census of October, 1933, Federal Emergency Relief Administration, Government Printing Office, Washington, D. C., Report Number One, p. 8.
[4] The Unemployment Relief Census of October, 1933, showed that 16.7 percent of the relief population was Negro, compared with 9.7 percent of the 1930 population. The same, p.7.

the proportion of Negroes in the transient relief population was somewhat smaller than their proportion in the total population of 1930, and only about half the proportion they represented in the total resident relief population. This seems to justify the conclusion that although proportionately the Negro population was more seriously affected by the depression than was the native white population, the Negro was much less inclined to seek a solution of his difficulties through transiency. Moreover, it must be remembered that in the South, where they are most numerous, local custom still tends to immobilize the Negroes.[1]

In connection with this discussion it is of interest to point out the markedly different color and nativity distribution reported by the resident homeless unattached in the six cities[2] where they received relief in transient bureaus. Table 4 shows that the proportions of native white persons among the resident homeless unattached were considerably smaller, and the proportions of foreign-born whites and other races, were much larger, than was the case with the unattached transients.

In his study of the resident homeless unattached in New York City, Nels Anderson[3] found that, depending on the social service agency studied, from 20 to 46 percent of the homeless were foreign born. If the proportions of foreign-born white and other races in Table 4 are combined for the resident homeless unattached, the results are not greatly unlike those found for New York City. Here, as was the case with age characteristics, is evidence that the resident homeless unattached as a group were distinctly different from the unattached transients.

Marital Status   1630580

The marital status of the transient relief population showed little variation from month to month. In each of the five months, December 1934 through April 1935, approximately 80 percent of the unattached transients were single, 10 percent widowed or divorced, 6 percent married, and 5 percent separated. Among the heads of family groups (i.e. the person responsible for each group) between 84 and 88 percent were married, approximately 7 percent were widowed or divorced, 6 percent separated, and 1 to 2 percent were single. (See Table 5, Appendix B.) Similar results were obtained from a tabulation of September 1934 registrations, which provided a classification of marital status by sex, age, and color and nativity.

---

[1] In this connection see Nelson Jackson, Negroes on the Road, State of New Jersey Emergency Relief Administration, January, 1935, page 8.
[2] For these cities see footnote 1, p. 28, Chapter II.,
[3] The Homeless in New York City, as cited above.

Sex and Marital Status. While only 12 percent of the 33,460 transient individuals[1] included in the September registrations in the thirteen study cities were females, significant differences between the marital status of males and females are apparent among both the unattached and heads of family groups. (See Table 6, Appendix B.)   Slightly more than four-fifths of the unattached men were single, in contrast with a little less than two-fifths of the unattached women; and the proportion of unattached women who were married, widowed, divorced, or separated, was from two to four times as large as was the case with unattached men. This suggests that the unattached women were somewhat older than the men.

The difference in marital status of men and women is likewise apparent among the heads of family groups; 95 percent of the male heads were married; in contrast with 22 percent of the female heads. On the other hand, 36 percent of the female heads were separated, and 34 percent widowed or divorced, in comparison with only 1 and 2 percent respectively for male heads. Apparently, broken homes were a factor in family group transiency. As to members of transient family groups other than the head, it was found that 98 percent of the males were single and 2 percent married. The high proportion of single males is accounted for by the number of boys under sixteen years of age. Among the females, 43 percent were single, 55 percent married, 1 percent widowed or divorced, and the same proportion separated; the single females were principally girls under 16 years of age.

Age and Marital Status. The single men among the unattached transients were younger than the group as a whole: 52 percent were under twenty-five years of age as compared with 44 percent of all unattached men.   The oldest group among the male unattached was found among the widowed or divorced, of whom 97 percent were twenty-five years of age or older, and 44 percent, forty-five years of age or older.   The separated males as a group were also slightly older than those reported as married. (See Table 7a, Appendix B.)

The single unattached women were likewise much younger than the group as a whole, and also younger than the single unattached men: 66 percent were under twenty-five years of age in comparison with 39 percent of all unattached women and with 52 percent

---

[1] The discussion of marital status by sex, age, and color and nativity makes use of a three-fold classification of the transient population: (1) unattached transients; (2) heads of transient family groups; and (3) members of family groups other than the head. The purpose of the third classification is to introduce at this convenient point a brief description of some of the personal characteristics of family group transients other than the head.

of the unattached men. A somewhat larger proportion of the unattached female widowed or divorced (49 percent) were forty-
five years of age or older than was the case with the unattached
males (44 percent); but the separated and married unattached
females tended to be younger than the unattached males of the
same marital status.

For both the unattached and heads of family groups the proportion of persons forty-five years of age or older was greater
among the women than among the men; and this finding is associated with a much higher proportion of widowed and divorced
among the women. (See Tables 7a and 7b, Appendix B.)

Among members of family groups other than the head, over
half were children under 16 years of age; and most of the remainder were married women (wives of family heads) whose ages
were somewhat younger than those of the married women who were
heads of family groups. (See Tables 7b and 7c, Appendix B.)

Color and Nativity and Marital Status. Among the unattached
transients single individuals predominated in each of the color
and nativity groups: The range was from 76 percent of the
foreign-born white to 86 percent of other races; while for the
largest color and nativity group, the native white, the proportion was 81 percent. Little variation was found in the proportion of each color and nativity group that was married: The
smallest proportion was 5 percent for the native white, and the
largest, 7 percent, for both the foreign-born white and the
Negroes. The most noticeable variation was found for the
widowed, divorced, and separated: 13 percent of the foreign-
born white were widowed or divorced, in contrast with only 7
percent of the Negroes, and 5 percent of other races. Negroes,
on the other hand, reported the largest proportion of separated
(8 percent), and other races, the smallest (3 percent). (See
Table 8a, Appendix B.)

. The largest proportion of married heads of family groups
was found among the native white (84 percent), and the smallest
proportion among the Negroes (66 percent). Both the Negro and
the foreign-born white reported a larger proportion (11 and 10
percent) of widowed or divorced heads of family groups than
did the native white (7 percent). Fifteen percent of the Negro
heads of family groups were separated, in contrast with but 7
percent of the native and foreign-born white. (See Table 8b,
Appendix B.)

Size of Transient Family Groups

The average transient family group was smaller by about one
person than the average relief family in the general population. During the period September 1934 through April 1935,

the average transient family group did not fall below 3.0 persons, nor exceed 3.2 persons; while the average size of the
sedentary relief family group, according to the Unemployment
Relief Census of October 1933, was 4.4 persons.[1] Table 9,
Appendix B, shows that about half of the transient families
each month consisted of two persons; that from one-fifth to
one-quarter consisted of three persons; and that large families
(six or more persons) were relatively few.

Although no tabulation was made of the composition of transient family groups, it is possible to infer something of their
composition from the data on size of families and marital status
of all members of family groups. Reference to the tables sup-
porting the discussion of marital status (Tables 7a to 9, Appendix B) shows the following information concerning family
groups registered during September 1934:

TOTAL PERSONS IN FAMILY GROUPS	6562
NUMBER OF FAMILIES	2122
AVERAGE SIZE	3.1
MARRIED MALES, FAMILY HEADS	1681
MARRIED FEMALES, NOT HEADS	1673
BOYS UNDER 16 YEARS OF AGE	1171
GIRLS UNDER 16 YEARS OF AGE	1179
TOTAL	5704
PERCENT OF ALL FAMILY GROUP PERSONS	87

Since about half of the family groups consisted of two persons
(Table 9), and since married male family heads were almost exactly equalled by married females who were not at the head of
the family group, it seems logical to assume that most of the
two person families consisted of husband and wife. Furthermore,
since children under 16 years of age accounted for most of the
family persons other than the approximately equal number of
married male heads and married female non-heads, it seems likely
that most transient family groups consisted either of husband
and wife, or of husband, wife, and one or more children under
sixteen years of age.

If this reasoning is correct, it tends to confirm what was
suggested by the age distribution of family group heads: That
transient families were, for the most part, younger married
couples with no, or few, children, that either had not established strong social and economic ties in their community or
were not sufficiently hampered by family obligations to prevent

---

[1] See the Unemployment Census of October, 1933, Federal Emergency Relief
Administration, Government Printing Office, Washington, D. C., Report
Number One, p. 9.

a migration in search of a more favorable environment.

Education

Measured in terms of school years completed, the transient
unemployed were a fairly well-educated group. A tabulation of
the school attendance history of unattached transients registered in the thirteen study cities during September 1934, shows
that only 2 percent had no schooling; 56 percent had terminated
their formal education upon completion of one to eight years of
grade school; 38 percent, upon completion of one to four years
of high school; and nearly 4 percent upon completion of one to
four years of college. Another index of the educational level
of unattached transients is the proportion whose education had
ended with the completion of each of the three divisions in the
educational system—grade school, high school, and college.[1]
The completion of grade school only was reported by 26 percent,
of high school only, by 13 percent, and of college by 1 percent
of the unattached transients. But perhaps the best indication
of the educational level of this group is that more than two-
thirds (68 percent) had at least a grade school education. (See
Table 10, Appendix B.)

Heads of transient family groups reported a slightly lower
level of schooling completed: 3 percent had no schooling, and
35 percent had left school without completing grade school, in
comparison with 2 and 30 percent respectively for the unattached
transients. However, the proportion of family heads that ended
their education with the completion of grade school, high school,
and college, was about the same as with the unattached transients,
which leaves the difference in educational level principally
the larger proportion that had left grade school before completion, and the smaller proportion that had attended high
school without completing the four years. Since the heads of
family groups were, on the whole, somewhat older than the unattached, this difference in schooling is in part the result of
the spread of compulsory school attendance and the improvement
in school facilities since the older transients were of school
age.

---

[1]These data were collected in terms of actual years of schooling completed
in grade school, high school, and college; but in this report grade school
is taken to consist of eight years, and high school and college of four
years each. The answer "completed grade school" was not accepted unless
it reported eight years of schooling. There were a few cases where grade
school had consisted of but six or seven years; and, although the individual reported the completion of grade school, the entry was the actual number of years completed. A similar procedure was followed in reporting high
school and college attendance.

The resident homeless unattached reported a lower level of schooling completed than did either the unattached transients or the heads of transient family groups: 6 percent of the homeless had completed no schooling; 43 percent had stopped short of the eighth grade; and only 23 percent had continued beyond grade school, in contrast with 42 percent of the unattached transients and with 37 percent of the heads of transient families. As in the case of the heads of family groups, the lower level of schooling among the resident homeless is associated with the older age of this group. Indeed, there appears to be a fairly consistent inverse relationship between age and schooling completed, among both the transient and the resident homeless eighteen years of age and older.

Although the unattached transients, the transient family heads, and the resident homeless differed as to the amount of schooling completed, there is close agreement in the proportion of those in each group whose education terminated at the completion of the eighth grade. This is apparent from Chart V, which shows the distribution of school years completed for each of the three groups, and from a comparison of the proportions of the three groups whose schooling terminated in each year. Completion of the eighth grade ended the schooling of 26 percent of the unattached, 25 percent of the heads of family groups, and 28 percent of the resident homeless. This pronounced concentration of the three distributions at the eighth grade affects the median school year completed, which is the eighth grade for each of the three groups. There are two circumstances which help to explain this particular concentration: (1) the spread of legislation making school attendance compulsory at least until the age of 14, and frequently until the age of 16; and (2) the known tendency of persons, out of pride or carelessness, to report the completion of grade school when they actually stopped somewhat short of that point.

Color ana Nativity and Education. There were distinct differences in the educational level of the several color and nativity groups. Among the unattached transients, the native whites reported the smallest percentage with no schooling completed, and the Negroes and Mexicans, the largest. (See Chart VI; and Table II, Appendix B.) The native white were the best educated of the color and nativity groups: 45 percent of them had continued their formal schooling beyond the eighth grade, in contrast with only 22 percent of both the foreign-born white and the Negroes, and with 19 percent of the Mexicans. The superiority of the native white in terms of schooling completed is likewise shown in the proportion of each color and nativity group that had a high school education or better: Native white,

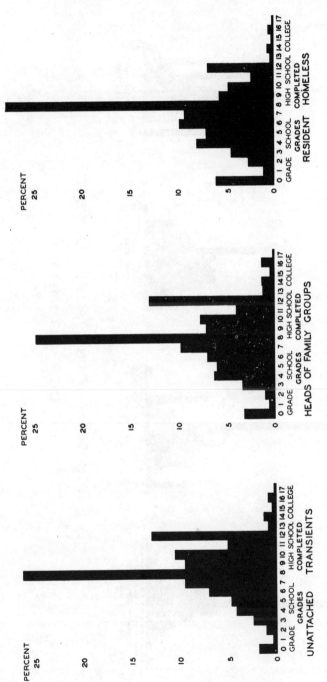

CHART V

SCHOOLING OF TRANSIENT AND RESIDENT HOMELESS

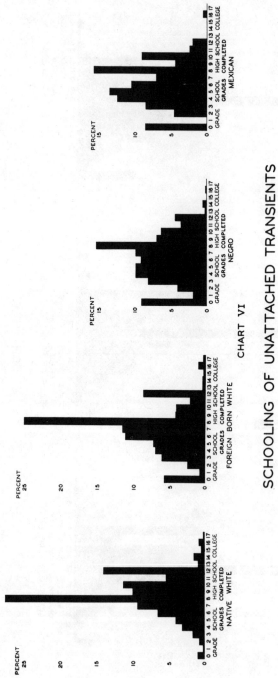

CHART VI

SCHOOLING OF UNATTACHED TRANSIENTS

BY COLOR AND NATIVITY

18 percent; foreign-born white, 12 percent; Negroes, 5 percent; and Mexicans, 3 percent.

The difference in educational level is shown by the median year of completed schooling, which was the eighth grade for the native white, the seventh grade for the foreign-born white, and the sixth grade for both the Negroes and the Mexicans; but, because the point of concentration falls within the grade school period, the median fails to show the differences in schooling among these color and nativity groups as clearly as do the shapes of the diagrams in Chart VI. This chart emphasizes the following facts: Among the native white group there is a marked concentration at the eighth grade, a large precentage of the cases above this point, and an important secondary peak at the twelfth grade. The foreign-born white group conforms fairly well to the native white, except that a larger proportion of the cases lie below the eighth grade. For the Negroes, the figure shows the least contrast among the percentages of those whose schooling ended during the grade school period. While the median year completed by Negroes was the sixth grade, the point of greatest concentration was, as in the case of the other color and nativity groups, the eighth grade. The figure representing the schooling completed by the Mexican groups is most irregular, and the most highly concentrated at the lower levels of grade school.

Age and Education. An analysis of the schooling completed by age groups reveals, for the unattached transients, some interesting facts which are consistent with expectations. The lowest age group, those under sixteen years of age, had the least educational experience. (See Table 12a, Appendix B.) Obviously they had not had time to complete as many years of schooling as had those in the older groups. The preponderance of cases in this group were in or near the fifteen-year age interval, which agrees with the finding that 65 percent of them had completed seven years or more of schooling.[1] (See Chart VII.) The proportion of those who had completed seven or more years of schooling increases to 83 percent for the sixteen-seventeen year group, and to 85 percent for the eighteen-nineteen year group. This latter group was, on the average, the best educated of any of the age groups in the population: less than 1 percent of them had failed to finish at least one year of schooling; and over one-half (53 percent) had completed one or more years of high school.

---

[1] Percentages for individual school years completed are shown only in graphic form on Chart VII. The percentages in Tables 12a and 12b are for the conventional groupings of school years—grade school, high school, and college.

However, the age group, twenty through twenty-four years, reported the largest percentage of high school graduates and the lowest percentage that failed to complete as much as eight years of schooling. In the higher age groups there is a gradual decrease in the proportion that had extended their formal education beyond the grade school period, despite the fact that the thirty-five through forty-four year group shows the highest percentage of college graduates.

A comparison of unattached transients with heads of family groups, by age groups and school years completed, shows that the unattached transients, twenty through twenty-four years of age, had a slightly better school record; that there was little difference in the schooling of unattached and heads of family groups who were twenty-five through forty-four years of age; and that the schooling of those forty-five years of age and older was less for the unattached transients than for the heads of family groups. (See Tables 12a and 12b, Appendix B.) The presence of a larger proportion of habitual transients among the unattached group probably accounts for their inferior educational rating when compared with that of the heads of family groups. This tendency for the educational level of the unattached to be lower in the older age groups was even more marked among the resident homeless unattached: The percentage of those with no schooling rose from 1.3 percent for the resident homeless, twenty-five through thirty-four years of age, to 9.1 percent for those forty-five years of age and older.

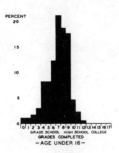

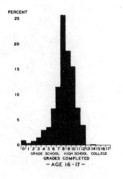
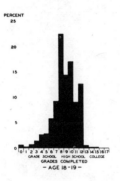
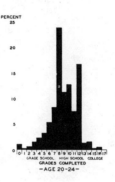

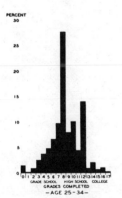
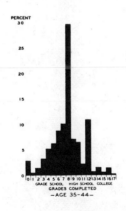
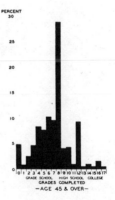

CHART VII

SCHOOLING OF UNATTACHED TRANSIENTS
BY AGE GROUPS

Chapter III

OCCUPATIONAL CHARACTERISTICS

More often than not, communities were divided in their atti-
tudes towards the transient. One view was that the transient,
by accepting lower wages, would replace resident workmen and
thereby increase the burden of local relief. The other view
held that the transient would not work under any circumstances,
and therefore was not entitled to assistance in the community.
The former view readily became the latter whenever the transient
refused to work for less than the prevailing wage; and the latter view persisted in many communities even after the Transient
Relief Program demonstrated that the transient would work.

The purpose of this chapter is to examine the occupational
characteristics of transients registered for relief in the thirteen cities included in the Research Section's study, and to
show something of their employment history before and during
migration. This examination is not designed to show that transients would work—for that has been clearly demonstrated in
transient camps and shelters; but to show what work they had
done in the past, and to throw some light on their prospects of
finding work in the future. Like the preceding chapter on personal characteristics, the emphasis will be upon statistical
description; but, unlike that chapter, the data are too detailed
to be summarized with any pretense at completeness. Although
some of the findings are summarized in the final section of this
report, they provide an inadequate statement of the occupational
characteristics of the transient relief population.

Employment Status. Almost without exception, unattached transients were unemployed at the time of registration for relief;
but the great majority was reported as both able and willing to
work[1]. During the seven-month period, October 1934 through
April 1935, the number of unattached transients who were employed[2] at the time of registration did not exceed one percent.
However, during six of the seven months, only 4 percent of the
unattached transients were reported as unable to work; and in
the remaining month (March 1935) the proportion was 3 percent.
(See Table 13, Appendix B.) The principal reasons given for

---

[1] This represents a judgment made by the interviewer at time of registration
for relief. Ability to work was determined largely upon such factors as
age and the absence of obvious or reported physical handicaps. Willingness
to work was based almost entirely upon the statement of the transient; but
these statements had to be consistent with data on age, previous employment
history, and willingness to participate in the work relief program of the
transient bureau.
[2] Those employed were either en route to a promised job, non-resident workers
on strike, or itinerant workers who were self-employed but in need of relief.

inability to work were temporary and permanent physical disabilities[1] and old age.

Among the heads of family groups a slightly higher proportion was employed at the time of registration, and a considerably larger proportion was unable to work than was the case with
the unattached transients. During the seven-month period considered, from 2 to 3 percent of the family heads were employed,
and from 7 to 11 percent were unable to work. (See Table 13,
Appendix B.) The larger proportion of family heads who were
unable to work, in comparison with unattached persons, was the
result of both a slightly larger proportion with physical disabilities, and the presence of women heads of family groups who
could not do gainful work because their time was devoted to the
care of the family.

When those who were unable to work are excluded, there remain
approximately 96 percent of the unattached persons, and from 89
to 93 percent of the heads of family groups, who were employable
in the sense that they were either unemployed but were considered able and willing to work, or were employed on the date of
registration. Similar results were obtained by the Division of
Transient Activities from a one-day survey, which included most
of the unattached men over eighteen years of age, and most of
the family group heads under care in the United States on June 3,
1935. The results of this survey are given below:

TABLE A.   EMPLOYABILITY OF TRANSIENTS UNDER CARE JUNE 3, 1935, AS REPORTED
BY THE DIVISION OF TRANSIENT ACTIVITIES, UNITED STATES TOTAL

	UNATTACHED MALES OVER 18	HEADS OF FAMILY GROUPS
ALL PERSONS	125,460	29,856
	Percent Distribution	
ALL PERSONS	100.0	100.0
EMPLOYABLE	92.2	90.7
UNEMPLOYABLE	7.8	9.3

A comparison of these returns with those given in Table 13
shows that they are substantially the same. The differences between the data from the Division of Transient Activities and those
from registrations in the thirteen cities during the seven-month
period probably arise from two circumstances: The Division of
Transient Activities excluded all male transients eighteen years
of age or younger—a highly employable group as far as physical
ability and willingness to work were concerned; and in the thirteen cities women heads of family groups were returned as unem-

---

[1] Temporary disabilities were physical handicaps that required medical attention, but were not likely to render the person unemployable for any
considerable period of time. Permanent disabilities were physical handicaps that, in all likelihood, rendered the person permanently unemployable for any type of work which would enable him to be self-supporting.

OCCUPATIONS OF GAINFUL WORKERS, RELIEF AND TRANSIENT POPULATIONS

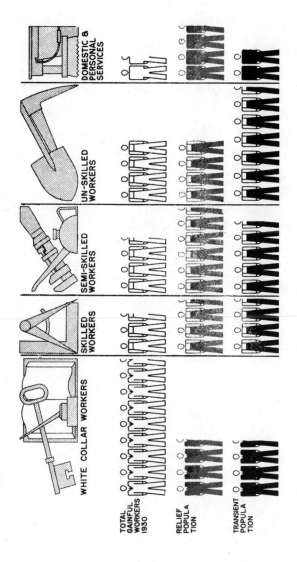

WHITE COLLAR WORKERS

SKILLED WORKERS

SEMI-SKILLED WORKERS

UN-SKILLED WORKERS

DOMESTIC & PERSONAL SERVICES

TOTAL GAINFUL WORKERS 1930

RELIEF POPULATION

TRANSIENT POPULATION

EACH OUTLINED FIGURE REPRESENTS 5% OF TOTAL GAINFUL WORKERS
EACH GRAY FIGURE REPRESENTS 5% OF TOTAL RELIEF POPULATION
EACH BLACK FIGURE REPRESENTS 5% OF TOTAL TRANSIENT POPULATION

DIVISION OF SOCIAL RESEARCH   AF-1502

ployable when the care of the family prevented their participation in gainful work—a procedure which tended to lower the proportion of family heads returned as employable.

While at first it may seem that the data both from the thirteen cities and from the country as a whole show, for a relief group, an unusually high proportion of employables, it must be remembered that the transient population was young, and that only the physically fit could stand the rigorous life on the road. It must also be remembered that employability is necessarily defined as the physical ability plus an expressed willingness to do gainful work, rather than as the probability of securing employment. Within the transient relief population was a considerable number of individuals between sixteen and twenty-five years of age who had never done gainful work but who certainly were physically able, and just as certainly were willing to work if they could find an employer who would overlook their lack of experience. There were likewise others—a smaller number—who had done gainful work in the past, but, because they had passed the age of forty-five years, were no longer considered employable at most jobs according to the standards of many employment offices.

For these reasons, it is necessary to examine in some detail both the work experience and the occupational characteristics of the transient relief population before a conclusion is reached as to their employability in terms of probability of reabsorption into private industry. This examination will be concerned with: I. The work history of transients, to determine the proportions with, and without, a usual occupation. II. Several broad groupings of those with usual occupations, to determine the economic levels from which the transient population was drawn. III. The detailed occupations subsumed under these groupings, to determine the variety of trades and pursuits usually followed by the transient unemployed. IV. Age and occupational characteristics, to determine the relationships between age, work history, and usual occupation.

   I. WORK HISTORY. When the work histories of unattached persons and heads of family groups are examined, without regard to age or sex, it is found that the proportion with no work experience was small. (See Table 14, Appendix B.) During the eight-month period, September 1934 through April 1935, only 3.8 to 5.3 percent of the unattached persons, and only 3.7 to 6.9 percent of the heads of family groups registered for transient relief in the thirteen cities, had never done gainful work. The variation from month to month seems to be the result of changes in the personnel of the transient population rather than because of any persistent increase in the number who had never been gainfully employed.

However, when those who had done gainful work are classified according to whether or not they had a usual occupation, it is found that the proportion with no usual occupation increased during the period examined. This increase was more marked among the unattached persons than among the heads of family groups. The percentage of unattached transients with no usual occupation increased steadily from 5.6 percent in September 1934, to 14.9 percent in April 1935; while the percentage of family group heads with no usual occupation increased from 1.1 percent in September 1934, to 5.4 percent in March, and to 4.7 percent in April 1935. One possible explanation of these increases is that the younger transients—those who reached working age during the depression years—were unable to obtain employment at any one trade or pursuit long enough to acquire a usual occupation, and in shifting about in search of work came to depend increasingly upon transient bureaus for assistance.

The work histories of men and women were tabulated separately for the four-month period, January through April 1935, to determine the differences attributable to sex. (See Table 15, Appendix B.) The most striking difference between the sexes is found among the heads of family groups: only about 1 percent of the male heads had never worked and about 95 percent had a usual occupation; while approximately 40 percent of the female heads had never worked, and less than 50 percent of them had a usual occupation. Among the unattached transients approximately 4 percent of the males had never worked, and more than 80 percent had a usual occupation; while about 25 percent of the females had never worked, and somewhat more than 60 percent had a usual occupation. It should be noted that male heads of family groups had a more favorable work history than did unattached males; while female heads of family groups had a less favorable work history than did unattached females. The older age of the male heads was the principal reason for their superior work history in comparison with the unattached males; while the care of the family group accounts for the inferior work history of the female heads in comparison with the unattached females.

II.   OCCUPATIONAL GROUPS. Broad groupings[1] of usual occupations[2] show that the proportion of unskilled and semi-skilled

---

[1]These groupings represent a special arrangement of the occupations reported by the Bureau of the Census in 1930 (see Fifteenth Census, Population, Vol. V, Table 3). The purpose of this arrangement is to show both the degree of skill represented by workmen included in this relief group, and the economic and social levels in the general population from which they came. A fairly detailed statement of the occupations included in each of these broad groups is provided in Table 19, Appendix B.

[2]The instructions for filling the schedule used in the Research Section's study of the transient relief population required that the usual occupation be determined as follows:
"For the purposes of this study, a usual occupation is: (1) The kind of work, craft, pursuit, occupation, etc., for which the registrant is best fitted as a result of training, practice, or personal aptitude. This is a judgment from the point of view of the interviewer. (2) The kind of work, etc., for which the registrant considers himself best fitted, for

workers in the transient relief population was higher than the
proportion of such workers in the general, or in the resident
relief population. During the four-month period, January through
April 1935, more than one-half of the unattached persons and
more than two-fifths of the heads of family groups who had a
usual occupation were classified as unskilled or semi-skilled
workers.[1] (See Table 16, Appendix B.) In addition, approximately 11 percent of the unattached persons, and approximately
8 percent of the heads of family groups, had usual occupations
classified in the servant and allied worker group, which is made
up almost entirely of unskilled and semi-skilled occupations.[2]
Combining the percentages of workers classified as unskilled,
semi-skilled, servants and allied workers, it is found that during the four-month period under consideration, about 65 percent
of the unattached persons and about 50 percent of the heads of
family groups had usually been employed at work of an unskilled
or semi-skilled nature.

   This difference between unattached persons and heads of family
groups in terms of skill extends throughout the occupational
groupings. In particular, the proportion of skilled workers,
proprietors, managers and officials, and professional persons
was consistently higher each month among the heads of family
groups than among the unattached persons. The difference is
equally evident from a comparison of the proportion of "white
collar"[3] workers in the two groups. Approximately 30 percent
of the family group heads registered during each of the four
months examined were "white collar" workers, in comparison with
approximately 17 percent of the unattached persons. These comparisons seem to justify the conclusion that heads of family
groups tended to come from a somewhat higher economic level in
the general population than did unattached persons.

   A comparison of the occupations of men and women shows that
the proportion of semi-skilled workers, and servants and allied
workers, was higher among the women than among the men. (See
Table 17, Appendix B.) The higher proportion of women with semi-
skilled occupations reflects the inclusion of semi-skilled

the same reasons enumerated in (1). This is a judgment from the point of
view of the registrant. (3) The kind of work the registrant followed for
the longest time. This is a judgment based on the work history of the
client. (4) The kind of work, etc., at which the registrant would probably
be employed, in the judgment of both the registrant and the interviewer,
if social and economic conditions were what is vaguely described as "nor-
mal". This is a judgment based on the factors enumerated in (1), (2), and (3).
[1] When the occupations of all gainfully employed persons in the United States,
as reported by the 1930 Census, are reduced to the same occupational groups,
it is found that 37.7 percent were reported as unskilled and semi-skilled.
(See Fifteenth Census, Population, Vol. V, Table 3). See Table 17, Appendix
B, for a comparison of transients with the gainfully employed population of
1930, and with a representative sample of the resident urban relief population of May 1934.
[2] See Table 19, Appendix B, for the specific occupations included in this and
other groups.
[3] As used here, "white collar" workers include those classified as: professional persons; proprietors, managers, and officials; clerical workers;
sales persons; semi-professional and recreational workers; and telephone,
telegraph, and radio operators.

operatives in laundries and dry-cleaning establishments where
women constitute a considerable part of the labor supply. The
proportion of women was also higher in three other occupational
groups: professional persons (principally nurses and school
teachers), clerical workers, and sales persons. On the other
hand, the proportion of men was noticeably higher in the skilled
and unskilled groups, and, to a lesser extent, in the proprietors,
managers, and officials group.

    III. USUAL OCCUPATIONS. [1] *Unskilled Workers.* Of the February
registrants who had a usual occupation, approximately 31 percent
of the unattached persons and 22 percent of the family group
heads were unskilled workers. (See Table 19, Appendix B.) In
each case, nearly one-half were farm laborers. Although practically all types of farming were represented, more than half of
the farm laborers had usually worked on the general, or unspe-
cialized, type of farm. Second to farm laborers in order of importance among the unskilled workers group were common laborers
(Laborers, not elsewhere classified). About 11 percent of the
unattached persons and 8 percent of the family group heads were
usually attached as common laborers to such industries as manu-
facturing, ·merchandising, public utilities, building and construction, service, etc. In addition to farm and common laborers,
the only other important group of unskilled workers was from the
mining and oil well industries—3 percent of the unattached
persons and 2 percent of the heads of family groups.

    Semi-skilled Workers. Occupations requiring some skill and
training were reported by 23 percent of the unattached and by 20
percent of the heads of family groups. Chauffeurs, delivery-
men, truck and tractor drivers comprised slightly under one-
third of this semi-skilled group, while slightly over one-third
were factory operatives. Semi-skilled workers in laundries and
dry cleaning establishments were classified as factory operatives.

    The balance of semi-skilled workers reported a wide variety
of occupations, with maritime employment the most important
among the unattached persons, and personal service employment
among the heads of family groups.

    Skilled Workers. About 17 percent of the unattached persons
and 20 percent of the heads of family groups were skilled manual

---

[1] Because of the great amount of detail, usual occupations are shown in extended form for only one month, February 1935, which was a fairly typical
month as indicated by a comparison with similar detailed tabulations for
other months.

workers. Well over half of each group were either building and
construction workers[1] or skilled mechanics. Skilled building
and construction workers represented 8 percent of the unattached
persons, and 9 percent of the heads of family groups, who had a
usual occupation. Among these workers, painters, paperhangers,
and carpenters occurred most frequently. If the skilled and unskilled building and construction workers are combined, it is
found that approximately 12 percent of both unattached persons
and heads of family groups were usually employed in the building and construction industry.

Servants and Allied Workers. About 11 percent of the unattached persons and 8 percent of the family heads were included
in the servant and allied worker group. About nine-tenths of
each group were domestic servants, waiters, or waitresses; the
remainder included bootblacks, charwomen, elevator tenders,
sextons, and porters. Although there were included a few skilled
and semi-skilled workers—such as chefs, cooks, and bartenders—
they were so few in number that there is little to distinguish
this group of occupations from those classified as unskilled.

Sales Persons. Slightly over 6 percent of the unattached
persons and somewhat less than 8 percent of the family group
heads were usually employed in the sale of goods and services.
Although this classification was designed to include sales persons in all lines of commercial activity, most of those included
had worked in retail stores. Among the several "white collar"
classifications, salespersons ranked first among the unattached
persons, and second among the family group heads.

Clerical Workers. While the percentages included in this
group are not large—5.3 percent for the unattached persons,
and 2.7 percent for the family group heads—it was the only one
of the "white collar" classifications in which unattached persons were proportionately more numerous than were heads of family groups. However, since general clerical workers were reported much more frequently than were such semi-skilled workers
as typists and stenographers, it would seem that this group does
not provide an exception to the conclusion that family group
heads represented a higher economic level in the general population.

Proprietors, Managers, and Officials. Agricultural proprietors and managers, and wholesale and retail dealers were most
important among proprietors, managers, and officials, who comprised nearly 15 percent of the heads of family groups, in contrast with only about 4 percent of the unattached persons. This
category presents the most marked occupational difference between
the unattached persons and the heads of family groups. However,

---

[1] Includes brick and stone masons and tile layers, carpenters, electricians,
painters and paper hangers, plasterers and cement finishers, plumbers and
gas and steam fitters, roofers and slaters, and structural iron workers.

it must be remembered that the family heads were, as a group,
somewhat older and therefore had more opportunity to rise to the
proprietary class. Moreover, the inclusion of tenant farmers in
the proprietary group tended to overweight this classification,
since the tenant farmer frequently represents a position in the
economic scale no better than that occupied by the common laborer.

*Professional Persons; Semi-professional and Recreational
Workers; Telephone, Telegraph, and Radio Operators.* The proportion of professional and technical persons in the transient
population was small. Among the February registrants, only 3
percent of the unattached and 5 percent of the heads of family
groups reported occupations falling under these three classifications, which include the more highly skilled of the "white
collar" pursuits.

IV. AGE AND OCCUPATIONAL CHARACTERISTICS. Age is no less
important in a discussion of the occupational characteristics of
the transient relief population than it was in the discussion of
personal characteristics. When the work histories and usual
occupations of transients registered in the thirteen cities during April 1935—a fairly typical month—are examined by age
groups,[1] significant variations are discovered. (See Tables 20a
and 20b, Appendix B.)

Never Worked. While only 3.3 percent of all unattached men
registered during April 1935 had never been gainfully employed,
this was true of 14.5 percent of those under twenty years of age,
and of less than 1 percent of those twenty-five years of age and
older. (See Table B. below.)

TABLE B.   PERCENT OF TRANSIENTS WHO HAD NEVER WORKED, APRIL 1935, REGISTRATIONS IN 13 CITIES

AGE GROUPS	UNATTACHED PERSONS		HEADS OF FAMILY GROUPS	
	MALE	FEMALE	MALE	FEMALE
TOTAL	3.3	25.1	0.5	35.4
UNDER 20 YEARS	14.5	40.5	-	(A)
20-24 YEARS	2.7	19.3	-	(A)
25-34 YEARS	0.9	15.7	0.7	38.9
35-44 YEARS	0.6	23.5	0.5	28.3
45 YEARS AND OVER	0.3	29.0	-	36.7

(A) PERCENTAGES NOT COMPUTED BECAUSE OF SMALL NUMBERS INVOLVED.

Among all unattached women, 25.1 percent had never been gainfully employed. Although the largest proportion without work
experience was reported by those under twenty years of age, the
second largest proportion was reported by those forty-five years

[1]Fewer age groups are used than in the presentation of age data in Chapter
1. The small proportion of unattached persons over forty-four years, and
of family group heads under twenty years, seems sufficient justification
for combining these age intervals to avoid too great detail. The full
age distributions from fifteen to sixty-four years may be found in Tables
2a and 2b, Appendix B.

of age, or older. Practically all of the male heads of family
groups had been gainfully employed; but somewhat over one-third
(36.4 percent) of the female heads of family groups had not.
   No Usual Occupation.   The most striking variation in work
histories among the age groups was found in the proportions with
no usual occupation. Among all unattached men, 15.0 percent had
no usual occupation; however, 51.0 percent of those under twenty
years of age had no usual occupation, compared with only 1.6 percent of those forty-five years of age and older. (See Table C,
below.)

TABLE C. PERCENT OF TRANSIENTS WHO HAD NO USUAL OCCUPATION, APRIL 1935, REGISTRATIONS IN 13 CITIES

AGE GROUPS	UNATTACHED PERSONS		HEADS OF FAMILY GROUPS	
	MALE	FEMALE	MALE	FEMALE
TOTAL	15.0	12.4	2.6	17.4
UNDER 20 YEARS	51.0	23.8	(A)	(A)
20–24 YEARS	19.9	11.9	8.6	(A)
25–34 YEARS	4.4	12.0	2.4	13.3
35–44 YEARS	2.3	9.9	1.1	19.4
45 YEARS AND OVER	1.6	6.5	-	16.7

(A) PERCENTAGES NOT COMPUTED BECAUSE OF SMALL NUMBERS INVOLVED.

A similar relationship was found between age and the lack of a
usual occupation for unattached women; but, probably because of
the greater proportion of unattached women who had never worked,
the inverse relationship was less extreme than in the case of
unattached men.   The proportion of men heads of family groups
with no usual occupation was much smaller, and the proportion
of women heads was slightly larger, than was true of unattached
men and women. The age group including the largest proportion
with no usual occupation was twenty to twenty-four years for
the men, and thirty-five to forty-four years for the women
heads of family groups.
   Skilled Workers. Although one-sixth of the unattached men,
and one-fifth of the male heads of family groups reported
skilled trades, it was the older, rather than the younger, men
who accounted for these proportions.   Only 2.8 percent of the
unattached men and one of the ten heads of family groups under
twenty years of age reported skilled occupations, in contrast
with 24.1 and 22.2 percent respectively for those forty-five
years of age and older. Women reporting skilled occupations
among both the unattached persons and heads of family groups
were too few to merit discussion by age groups.
   Semi-skilled Workers. Somewhat over one-fifth of the men
and one-quarter of the women reporting a usual occupation were
classified as semi-skilled workers. Age differentials were
less marked here than in some of the other occupational classifications.   Among the unattached men the highest proportion
of semi-skilled workers was found in the age group twenty to

twenty-four years; while for the male heads of family groups
the proportion was slightly higher in the age group twenty-
five to thirty-four years. Among the women, both unattached
persons and heads of family groups, the proportion of semi-
skilled workers was highest among those forty-five years of
age or older.

Unskilled Workers. One-third of the unattached men, and
slightly over one-fifth of the male heads of family groups,
with usual occupations, were unskilled. An examination of the
age distribution of these unskilled workers shows that, while
the point of greatest frequency was under twenty-five years of
age, there was a second point of concentration above forty-four
years of age. Thus among the unskilled men in the transient
relief population there were some who reached working age during the depression years, and who probably had little opportunity
to secure anything but intermittent employment at unskilled
pursuits; and there were still others who had passed through
the most active years of their working life without acquiring
any special occupational skill. The proportion of women reported as unskilled workers was too small to warrant discussion by age groups.

Servants and Allied Workers. An examination of the age distributions of men and women in this occupational group shows
that for neither sex is there any consistent relationship between age and the proportion reporting servant and allied pursuits. As might be expected, the proportion of women who were
usually employed as servants and allied workers was considerably
larger than the proportion of men.

Sales Persons. At first sight, there seems no logical explanation for the fact that among both the unattached men and women and the male heads of family groups, the proportions that
were returned as sales persons were higher among the younger,
than among the older age groups. However, when it is remembered
that sales persons include those who work for commission only,
as well as those who receive wages for their work, an explanation is suggested.   Even when unemployment was at a peak, the
help-wanted section of every newspaper contained advertisements
for salesmen on commission; and it seems probable that this
type of employment was all that could be obtained by some of
the transients, particularly the younger individuals who had
no previous experience in gainful employment.

Clerical Workers. Clerical workers were proportionately
most numerous in the age group twenty to thirty-four years. In
proportion to their number in the transient population, women
reported clerical occupations much more frequently than did
men; this was true of both unattached transients and heads of
family groups. It is not surprising to find a greater proportion of women in this category, since the proportion of women

in the general population who were returned as clerical workers
was more than three times the proportion of men.[1]

Proprietors, Managers, and Officials.   There was evident a
direct relationship between age and the proportion of transients classified as proprietors, managers, and officials.   In
the first place, there was a marked increase in the proportions
of men and women proprietors, managers, and officials (both
unattached persons and heads of family groups) as age increased.
For instance, 1 percent of the unattached men and 8.5 percent
of the male heads of family groups under twenty-five years of
age were included in this category, in contrast with 6.9 and 26.4
percent, respectively, of those forty-five years of age and older.
In the second place, the proportion of proprietary workers was
higher for heads of family groups than for unattached transients, even in the same age groups.

Duration of Employment at Usual Occupation.   Data showing
the duration of last employment of unattached persons and of
family group heads at their usual occupation before beginning
migration will throw some light on the occupational stability
of transients while they were still a part of the resident population.   In addition, this information will be pertinent to
an appraisal of their employability.

In each of the three months, February through April 1935,
somewhat over half of both the unattached persons and heads of
family groups with a usual occupation had worked at it for periods of eighteen months or longer during their last employment
before migration.   Last employment at usual occupation of less
than six months' duration was reported by approximately 18 percent of both unattached persons and heads of family groups;
and last employment of six through seventeen months' duration
was reported by about 27 percent of the unattached persons and
24 percent of the heads of family groups.[2]   (See Table 21,
Appendix B.)

Very few of either the unattached persons or heads of family
groups had come directly into the transient relief population
at the termination of the last employment at their usual occupation. Many of them had been totally unemployed for some time
before migration;   and others had worked occasionally at jobs
other than their usual occupation.   However, the data on duration of last job at usual occupation before migration seem to
provide sufficient justification for the   conclusion that at
least a majority of the transient unemployed had stable work
histories before beginning migration.

---

[1] See Fifteenth Census, Population, Vol. V, Table 3.
[2] The time intervals used in Table 21, Appendix B, to show duration of employment were chosen to represent relatively short, intermediate, and
long periods of employment.

Employment During Migration. It will be shown in a later
section of this report that search for work was the reason
given most frequently by transients to explain their presence
in the transient relief population. At this point it is possible to determine what proportion of the transient population
was successful in obtaining employment during migration, and
something of the duration and nature of the jobs secured.

During the three-month period February through April 1935,
only about one-third of the unattached persons, and two-fifths
of the heads of family groups registered for relief in the
thirteen cities, had secured one or more non-relief[1] jobs
during migration. Moreover, most of the employment secured
during migration was of a temporary nature. Of the unattached
persons who secured any employment during migration, nearly
one-quarter reported that their first job lasted less than
fifteen days; and well over half reported that their first job
lasted less than two months. (See Table 22, Appendix B.) Even
though the heads of family groups were somewhat more successful
in securing employment during migration than were unattached
persons, the duration of the employment was much the same. The
principal difference was a slightly larger percentage of family
heads who secured jobs of three to twelve months' duration. Of
the unattached persons and heads of family groups who secured
employment during migration less than half found more than one
job; and when the duration of the last of two or more jobs was
tabulated, the results did not differ materially from those
secured for the first job. In summary, it may be said that at
the time of registration for relief less than half of the transients had secured any employment during their wanderings, and
that most of the employment that was secured was of a temporary
nature. Therefore, it seems evident that transiency did not
provide a solution for unemployment. This becomes even more
evident from a comparison of the usual occupations before migration with the jobs secured during migration.

Casual and Non-casual Occupations. During the period October
1934 through April 1935, the usual occupations of transients
before migration included a small, and the jobs secured during
migration a large, proportion of casual pursuits.   (See Table
23a, Appendix B.) By casual is meant those short-time seasonal
employments in such industries as agriculture, forestry, fish-
ing, mining, and construction, which depend to some extent upon
a mobile labor supply; and, more specifically, such occupations
as harvest hand, berry picker, woodsman, clam-digger, and unskilled manual occupations in mining and construction industries. During the seven months examined, only about 5 percent

---

[1] Employment during migration was defined as "non-relief employment lasting
three days or longer for wages."

of the unattached persons reported usual occupations before
migration that were of a casual nature; while of those who obtained employment during migration, from 37 to 45 percent reported casual pursuits as the first job of three days or longer,
and from 42 to 54 percent reported casual pursuits as the last
of two or more jobs. Among the heads of family groups the proportion whose usual occupation before migration was of a casual
nature was much the same as in the case of the unattached (see
Table 23b, Appendix B); but of those who obtained employment
during migration, the proportion reporting casual pursuits was
considerably smaller than was found for the unattached.   Thus
it appears that not only were the heads of family groups more
successful in obtaining employment during migration than were
the unattached, but also that they depended less upon casual
pursuits.
    Employability. The description of the occupational characteristics of the transient relief population should throw
some light on the proportion of this mobile relief group that
is most likely to obtain private employment as the demand for
labor increases with industrial recovery. It is believed that
the majority of the transient relief population preferred permanent employment and a community life to a migratory existence
and transient relief. This belief is supported by the material
presented in the discussion of usual occupations, particularly
the data on the duration of last employment at the usual occupation before migration.
    When the employment status of unattached persons and heads
of family groups was discussed (see page 45), it was noted
that the large proportion reported as employable was a reflection
of ability and expressed willingness to work rather than the
probability of securing private employment. Undoubtedly some
of those reported by the transient bureaus as employable were
too old to be readily absorbed by private industry; others
were handicapped by partial disabilities, and lack of work
experience or usual occupation. This suggests that the data
on ability and expressed willingness to work overstate the employability of the transient relief population; and that employability should now be considered in view of such factors as age
and work history, as well as employment status on the day of
registration for relief.
    Because of the large proportion of unskilled and semi-skilled
workers in the transient relief population, age would seem to
be one of the most important factors conditioning employability,
although it is difficult to set the limits at which employability is affected by age. Private employment offices are
inclined to question the employability of the unskilled or semi-skilled worker who is unemployed and over forty-five years of

age; and the unemployed youth under sixteen is likely to find his lack of experience a handicap as long as the labor market is over-supplied with workers of some experience. It would seem, therefore, that the most readily employable group in the transient relief population would be found among those unattached persons and heads of family groups who were sixteen to forty-five years of age.

Reference to Tables 2a and 2b, Appendix B, shows that during the twelve-month period (May 1934 through April 1935) 84 to 88 percent of the unattached persons and 78 to 82 percent of the heads of family groups registered in the thirteen cities were sixteen to forty-five years of age. Since the variation from month to month is not large, the April 1935 data will be used in considering the proportion of the transient relief population that was most readily employable.

During April, 86 percent of the unattached persons and 79 percent of the heads of family groups were sixteen to forty-five years of age. When the employment status of registrants during April is examined by age groups, it is found that 2 percent of the unattached persons and 7 percent of the heads of family groups were sixteen to forty-five years of age and unable to work.[1] This leaves 84 percent of the unattached persons and 72 percent of the heads of family groups who could be considered readily employable as far as the criteria designated for age, ability, and expressed willingness to work are concerned.

However, some of these transients had never done gainful work, and others had never worked long enough at any pursuit to acquire a usual occupation.[2] When employability is measured in terms of physical ability and expressed willingness to work, lack of experience or the absence of a usual occupation cannot be considered a handicap; but when employability is considered in terms of probability of obtaining private employment in an overcrowded labor market, some allowance must be made for these factors. Among the April 1935 registrants, 3.6 percent of the unattached persons and 4.6 percent of the heads of family groups were sixteen to forty-five years of age and had never been gainfully employed; while 14.7 and 4.3 percent, respectively, had worked, but had not acquired a usual occupation. Obviously it is impossible to determine the extent to which lack of work experience or a usual occupation is a handicap in

---

[1] Employment status on the date of registration is shown by months in Table 13, Appendix B; but this table does not show age data. The percentages used in this paragraph were obtained by sorting the registration cards of all persons sixteen to forty-five years of age according to ability to work. Since only part of the April registrations were considered, the results are shown only in the text.

[2] For a description of the factors determining the designation of a usual occupation, see footnote 2, page 46.

securing private employment. Nevertheless, it seems important
to show that these factors existed, and that they will have a
bearing on the employability of the transient relief population
in terms of absorption by private industry.

It would be possible, from the data presented earlier in
this chapter, to consider still other factors such, for instance, as occupational skills,   which condition the ready employability of transients. But the purpose of this reconsider-
ation of employability is not to attempt an exact numerical
statement of the more employable part of the transient relief
population. Instead, the purpose is to show that factors other
than ability and willingness to work have an important bearing
on the absorption of transients by private industry. It would
seem that the absorption of even the more employable part of
the transient relief population depends to a considerable extent upon a marked increase in the demands of industry for unskilled and semi-skilled workers.[1] Considering the large number of such workers in the resident relief population,[2] it
seems probable that the absorption of semi-skilled and unskilled
workers, whether resident or transient, will be slow. Under
these circumstances, the prospects for the employment of the
less employable part of the transient relief population are not
encouraging; and it may be expected that many of them will continue their wanderings and depend on seasonal and casual employment for subsistence, or become part of the resident homeless population of our large cities.

---

[1] See Table 20b, Appendix B, for a classification of usual occupations by
age groups.
[2] See occupational distribution of the resident relief population in 79
cities, May 1934, Table 17, Appendix B.

Chapter IV

ORIGIN AND MOVEMENT OF THE TRANSIENT RELIEF POPULATION

In the discussions of personal and occupational character-istics of transients, little has been said of their reasons for migration; and nothing, of their origin and destination. It is the purpose of this chapter to consider specific reasons for depression transiency, the length of time that transients re-mained on the road, and the origins and destinations of this mobile relief group.

Reasons for Beginning Migration

The most frequent reason for the depression migration of needy persons and family groups was unemployment; but there were other reasons, such as ill health, search for adventure, domestic trouble, and inadequate relief, that were important factors in the formation of the transient relief population. When an attempt is made to present the reasons for the migra-tion of the thousands of cases registered in the thirteen cities, a serious difficulty is encountered: It is seldom that a single reason provides an adequate explanation of the pres-ence of the individual, or family group, on the road. But it is impracticable, if not impossible, to present in statistical form an account of all the factors involved in each case. Therefore, resort was had in the Research Section's study of transients to the device of reporting for each case only the most important of the reasons for transiency; that is, when two or more reasons could be given, the one was selected with-out which the person would presumably have remained a part of the resident population.[1]

Take, for instance, the case of a boy nineteen years of age who first reported that his reason for migration was to find work. From his educational record it was found that he had completed high school less than a year before registration for relief; and from his occupational history that he had never had permanent employment. Careful interviewing disclosed: (1) the fact that he had tried to find work in his home community, but had been unsuccessful; (2) that he had always wanted to see the Pacific Coast country; and (3) that he had an uncle living near San Francisco who might help him find a job. The interviewer had to choose one of three possible entries on the registration card: (1) Seeking work; (2) Adventure; (3) Visits. If, in the

---

[1] In the thirteen cities studied by the Research Section, a trained inter-viewer questioned each applicant for relief as to his reasons for begin-ning migration. The reason or reasons given were checked for consistency with such information as age, schooling, occupational history, and time of beginning migration. The reason selected and reported in each case was the one that best agreed with all of the facts obtained.

ORIGIN OF MIGRATION COMPARED WITH DISTRIBUTION OF TOTAL POPULATION

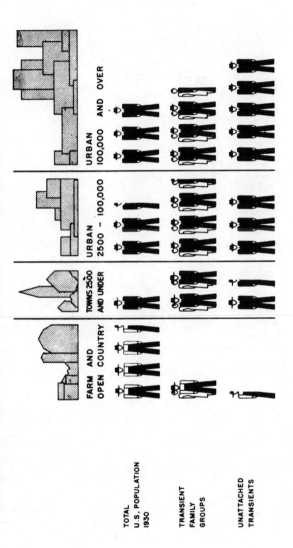

EACH GRAY FIGURE REPRESENTS 10% OF TOTAL U.S. POPULATION
EACH GROUP FIGURE REPRESENTS 10% OF FAMILY GROUPS
EACH BLACK FIGURE REPRESENTS 10% OF UNATTACHED TRANSIENTS
TRANSIENTS REGISTERED FOR RELIEF IN 13 CITIES, NOVEMBER 1934.

DIVISION OF SOCIAL RESEARCH   AF-1503

interviewer's judgment, the presence of the uncle was the fact without which the boy would probably have remained at home, the reason reported was "Visits". Otherwise, a choice had to be made between "Seeking work" and "Adventure", on a basis of their importance in explaining the fact of migration.

Although this procedure resulted in an over-simplified statement of reason for migration, by reporting in each case only one when there may have been several causes, it did provide a reliable indication of the order of importance among the principal reasons for transiency during the depression period. Moreover, it is possible to supplement and illustrate the statistical statement of reason for migration by abstracts from case histories obtained from special studies, or from the case work departments of the transient bureaus.[1] The reasons for migration reported by unattached persons and heads of family groups registered for relief in thirteen cities, October 1934 through April 1935, are presented in Tables 24a and 24b, Appendix B; and abstracts from a number of typical case histories are presented in Appendix B. The discussion which follows will be concerned with a brief examination of the reasons for the depression migration of unattached persons and family groups.[2]

Seeking work. Search for employment was by far the most important reason for the migration of both unattached persons and family groups. During the period October 1934 through April 1935, the principal reason for the migration of from 69 to 75 percent of the unattached persons and 65 to 68 percent of the heads of family groups registered for relief in thirteen cities was "seeking work".

For some of the unattached persons and heads of family groups this reason was not only the principal, but, as far as could be determined, the sole reason for migration. This was true of those individuals and family groups who seemed to have formed no attachment for any place or community, and who seemed to feel that one place was as good as another so long as employment could be obtained. It seems probable that such persons comprised a minority of those transients whose principal reason for migration was seeking work.

For the remainder, migration for the purpose of seeking employment was apparently a last resort after every attempt at

[1] Most of the case histories refer to transients registered in the thirteen cities studied by the Research Section; but occasionally use has been made of a case history from a city not included.
[2] The discussion of reason for migration refers specifically to transients registered in the thirteen study cities during the period October 1934 through April 1935. References to the thirteen cities and to Tables 24a and 24b have been omitted from the discussion to avoid undue repetition.

obtaining the necessities of a stable existence had failed.
Included in this category were those whose small savings had
been lost in closed banks or in business ventures, or spent in
maintaining a home in the hope that economic conditions would
improve; those who had not, for one reason or another, accumulated any reserves against unemployment; and those whose
friends and relatives were either unable or unwilling to extend or continue assistance that would enable the individual
or family to remain in the community. In not a few instances,
a search for work in some other place was the only alternative
to "going on relief" in a community where the person had lived
for many years as a self-supporting citizen. A careful reading of many case histories of transients suggests strongly
that "seeking work" as a reason for depression transiency is an
adequate explanation only for those who had no, or few, social
ties in the community. (See Case History Abstracts Nos. 1 to
5, Appendix C.)

Promised Job. The definite promise of a job in a specific
place was responsible for the migration of 2 to 3 percent of
the unattached persons and 4 to 6 percent of the heads of family groups. The distinction between this category and that of
seeking work was that in the one case the migrant had fairly
definite assurance that work could be obtained, while in the
other case, such assurance was lacking.

The more frequent instance of migration because of a promised
job came to the attention of the transient bureau because the
person had reached his destination, but had not secured the
job. However, this category also included those who were en
route to a promised job, but lacked the funds necessary for
the journey. (See Case History Abstracts Nos. 6 and 7, Appendix C.)

Adventure. The peculiar compound of restlessness and active
desire to extend the area of experience which is suggested by
the word wanderlust, was reported as the principal factor in
the migration of 7 to 8 percent of the unattached persons, but
of only a negligible percentage of the family groups. Among
the unattached transients this reason ranked next in importance
to seeking work as an explanation of transiency. Considering
the youth of the unattached transient population, it seems
more than likely that the percentage of persons included in the
category of adventure was an understatement, and that a more
detailed examination than was possible in this study would have
materially increased the proportion at the expense of those
classified as seeking work. (See Case History Abstract No. 8,
Appendix C.)

It seems probable that the applicant for relief from a service designed to relieve the hardships of the mobile unemployed

would have been inclined to stress the more obvious and understandable factor of unemployment rather than the intangible and easily misunderstood motive of adventure. Indeed, in reading the case histories of some of the younger transients who were reported as having migrated for a reason other than adventure, there is a strong implication that, whether they knew it or not, the desire to get away from the home environment with all its restrictions, and to see for themselves the cities and the areas known only by repute, was at least of equal importance with the reason reported. This was probably true of some of the older unattached persons as well, and of more of the family groups than the small percentage shown in Table 24b, Appendix B.

Ill Health. Two percent of the unattached persons and from 10 to 12 percent of the heads of family groups reported that their migration was for the purpose of finding a more favorable climate, or for obtaining medical aid because of some physical ailment.   Included in this category were those who went to Colorado, New Mexico, and Arizona because of pulmonary disorders; those who were advised, or had become convinced of their own accord, that they would benefit from the warmer climate of Southern California or Florida; and those who hoped to obtain for themselves or for some other member of the family group, hospitalization or medical attention which could not be obtained in their home community.   (See Case History Abstract No. 9, Appendix C.)

Among the family groups, ill health ranked next in importance to seeking work as a reason for migration; and it was frequently the ill health of a child or an aged parent rather than that of the head of the family group that was responsible for the migration.   The migrant in search of health, like the adventurous youth, is to be found on the road in good times and bad; and it is a debatable question whether their number increases or decreases during an economic depression.

Migratory Occupations. The reason for migration necessarily applied to the time when the person or family group left the last place in which a stable residence had been maintained. As a result, only 3 to 5 percent of the unattached persons, and from 1 to 3 percent of the family groups were reported as having begun migration because of migratory occupations. Actually, the percentages of both groups that were confirmed migratory workers at the time of registration for relief were much higher; but it was impossible to tell just when the individual ceased to be an unemployed person in search of work and became a permanent addition to the mobile labor supply that follows the harvests in the wheat belt, helps to pick the fruit and berry crops from Florida to the State of Washington, works in the lettuce fields of Arizona, the hop fields of California and Oregon, and the beet fields of Colorado and Minnesota. However, agriculture was not the only industry that afforded employment to the migratory workers included in the transient relief population. Seasonal employments in the lumber, canning, construction, mining, and shipping industries were some of the more frequent entries in the occupational histories of transients who were confirmed migratory workers at the time of registration for relief. (See Case History Abstracts Nos. 10 to 13, Appendix C.)

However, there are some occupations that are so definitely migratory that they can be designated arbitrarily as the reason for migration. For instance, the sailor who signs for employment from port to port, the carnival worker who "joins up", for the season, the peddler who wanders from place to place, and the itinerant minister who presides at revivals—all these and similar pursuits are migratory occupations from the day of adoption. As such they are readily identified as the reason for migration. The other and larger group of migratory workers included among the transient relief population apparently began migration in search of stable employment, and only by imperceptible degrees came to depend entirely upon the short-time seasonal employment as a means of existence. Therefore, the number of migratory workers among the transient relief population was inaccurately reported by the number of individuals and family groups whose reason for migration at time of starting was to follow migratory pursuits.

Domestic Difficulties. Difficulties within the home, or conflicts with relatives, were responsible for the transiency of 3 to 4 percent of the unattached persons and from 2 to 4 percent of the family groups. Among the unattached persons for whom this reason was reported was the runaway boy who had quarreled with one or both of his parents; the married person who had lost husband or wife through death, divorce, or desertion; and the son or daughter whose family had been broken up by death or incompatibility. In addition, there was the family that had lived with, or had been economically dependent upon, the family of the husband or wife, and had left because of a quarrel; the family that had lost one parent by separation, death, or divorce; and, not infrequently, the common-law family where the man or woman, or both, were not legally separated from the deserted spouse. (See Case History Abstracts Nos. 14 to 16, Appendix C.)

It is impossible to determine whether or not migration for the reasons reported as "domestic difficulties" was increased by depression conditions. The long experience of social service agencies with this type of migrant would seem to be justification for including domestic difficulties with adventure and ill health as reasons that are responsible for migration, more or less independently of economic conditions.

Inadequate Relief. Resident relief grants that were considered inadequate by the recipient were given as the reason for migration by 1 to 3 percent of the unattached persons and 2 to 4 percent of the heads of family groups. This category also includes persons who claimed that they were unable to obtain relief in any form. (See Case History Abstracts, Nos. 17 and 18, Appendix C.)

Although it is believed that unemployment relief grants had the effect of immobilizing the relief population, there were exceptions where just the reverse was true. When the standard of relief was actually, or reputedly, higher in one State than in an adjoining State, the differential was an inducement that attracted a small number of individuals and family groups. The substitution of work for direct relief was occasionally followed by a minor movement of persons who claimed that they were unable to obtain work relief employment. There were also instances of purely local migrations in the areas close to State boundaries. For example, during the winter of 1934 the Memphis transient bureau reported that Arkansas farm laborers were crossing the Mississippi River and applying for relief as transients; and Chicago, Illinois, at one time refused to accept transients from Gary, Indiana, just across the State line. Still another type of migrant included in the classification of inadequate relief was the unattached person who claimed that relief in his locality was refused to persons without dependents.

However, the number of persons that migrated because of inadequate relief in the home community was small; and these cases were exceptions to the general rule that persons once on resident relief were reluctant to forfeit their status for the chance of obtaining a higher standard of relief in some other locality.

Visits. When the reasons for migration were examined, it was found that some of the unattached persons and family groups were in the transient relief population because they had set out to visit a relative or friend, without having sufficient funds for the journey. There were also cases where the person to be visited could not be found, or had died. These and similar circumstances were responsible for the transiency of 3 to 4 percent of the unattached persons and 4 to 5 percent of the family groups. (See Case History Abstracts Nos. 19 and 20, Appendix C.)

Personal Business. Migration for the purpose of settling some business matter was reported by 1 percent of the unattached persons and 1 to 4 percent of the heads of family groups. The business matters included such items as an attempt to obtain compensation for war-time injuries, the disposal of real estate, a claim for damages from some public or private corporation, and the settlement of the estate of a deceased relative. (See Case History Abstracts Nos. 21 and 22, Appendix C.)

Other Reasons. Any plan of classifying reasons for migration necessarily required a residual category into which cases could be put that failed to come under any of the more readily determined categories, and yet were not reported frequently enough to justify a separate classification. Included as "other reasons" were such cases as the person released from a penal agency, an asylum, or similar public institution; the person who was avoiding some civil or criminal process of law; and those who, like the mentally defective and the chronic hobo, could give no satisfactory reason for their presence on the road.

In concluding this discussion of reasons for migration, it is important to point out what may already be obvious, that depression transiency was not a simultaneous mass-migration in response to a single cause or group of causes. Instead, it was the reaction of the individual to a particular set of circumstances in his own environment; and the point in time at which the reaction took the form of a migration varied both with the individual and with the force of the circumstances. Therefore, the transient relief population was constantly receiving additions from the resident population, and as a result was composed, during any one month, of persons who had been on the road for varying periods of time.

If these month-to-month additions to the transient population had been cumulative during the depression years, that is, if there had been no withdrawals, the population would have grown steadily in size, and the proportion that had been on the road for, say, six months or longer would have increased with time. Had this been the case, it would mean that one effect of the depression was the creation of a large body of transient and homeless persons who had exchanged sedentary for migratory habits and customs. It is therefore important to examine the length of time that transients had been on the road at the time of registration for relief, the rate at which transients were added to the population, and whatever evidence exists as to withdrawals from the population.

Duration of Migration

If the monthly rate of addition to the transient relief population be defined as the percentage of newcomers that registered for relief within the same month they began migration, it may be said that the rate varied from 15 to 21 percent for the unattached persons, and from 11 to 16 percent for the family

groups.   (See Table 25, Appendix B.)   These rates were obtained from the registrations in the thirteen study cities
during the seven-month period October 1934 through April 1935.

Apparently the rate of addition varied with the season of
the year, much as did registrations.   (See Charts I, II, and
III, Chapter 1, for registrations.) Nineteen percent of the
unattached persons registered during October 1934 began migration during that month; during November, the proportion declined to 17 percent, and in December, to 15 percent, which was
the low point. During the first four months of 1935, the rates
of addition were: January, 18 percent; February, 17 percent;
March, 21 percent; and April, 20 percent.

The variation in the rate of addition of family groups was
less closely related to the season of the year than was the
case with unattached persons.   However, the rate for family
groups was lower in January and February 1935, than in the
fall of 1934, or in March and April 1935. It should be noted
as significant of the difference between unattached and family
group transients, both as to mobility and the importance of the
break with community life, that the rate of addition for unattached persons was higher than that for the family groups in
six of the seven months, and in the remaining month the rates
were the same.

Leaving aside for the moment the question of whether these
monthly rates of addition were representative of the entire
period[1] that the Transient Relief Program was in operation,
either for the thirteen cities or for the country as a whole,
it is still possible to demonstrate that the size of the transient relief population was checked by withdrawals that at
times exceeded accessions.   For instance, assuming that the
rate of addition for the country as a whole was not unlike the
rate in the thirteen cities during the seven months for which
data are available, it is apparent that the transient population would have doubled in size if there had been no withdrawals.[2] (See Table 25, Appendix B.) Yet during this period
the number of unattached transients decreased in four, and the
number of family groups in two, of the seven months; and for
both groups the number of registrations in the seventh month

---

[1] A period, so far as additions were concerned, of a little more than two
years, July 1933 to September 1935.   Intake was ordered discontinued
in all States on September 20, 1935; but intake had been on a restricted
basis for several months prior in some States.

[2] Had the population actually doubled, the increase could have occurred
either in registrations, indicating increased mobility, or in cases under
care (mid-monthly census), indicating decreased mobility. See discussion
of mobility, pp. 68-74   for proof that changes in mobility were
largely independent of rates of addition, and that, therefore, withdrawals
afford the only explanation of the fact that the size of the population did
not increase as rapidly as is indicated by the rates of addition.

was less than the number in the first month. This seems sufficient justification for the conclusion that during this period the rate of withdrawal was at least equal to, and probably was in excess of, the rate of addition.

Returning to the question of whether the rates of addition in the thirteen cities were representative, it may be noted that they refer to a period when registrations in the thirteen cities and in the country as a whole were declining (October 1934 through February 1935) as well as when they were rising (March and April 1935). Since there are no reasons for believing that the transients registered for relief in the thirteen cities were unique as to the length of time they had been on the road, it is possible to use the rates of addition in these cities as a sufficient demonstration of the changing personnel of the transient relief population for the country as a whole.

The rates of addition do not indicate the length of time that transients remained on the road. However, this may be determined approximately by computing the proportion of each month's registrants that had begun migration within certain periods of time prior to the month of registration. The proportion that had been on the road for one month or less has already been shown as the monthly rate of addition. Considering next those that had begun migration sometime within the six months preceding and including the month of registration, it is found that the proportion varied from 57 to 63 percent for the unattached persons and from 53 to 61 percent for the family groups. (See Table 25, Appendix B.) The decline in the proportion of both groups that had been on the road for six months or less during each of the seven months examined, was almost exactly offset by an increase in the proportions that had been on the road for seven to twelve months at the time of registration. When the proportions for the two periods (six months or less, and seven to twelve months) are combined to obtain the proportion that had been on the road one year or less, the results are found to be: 75 to 78 percent for the unattached persons, with five of the seven months showing 77 percent; and 78 to 80 percent for the family groups, with three of the seven months showing 79 percent. These remarkably constant results were obtained during a period when both monthly registrations and rates of addition were much more variable.

These results lead to the conclusion that for the greater part of the transient relief population, the period of transiency was of relatively short duration. Apparently, a brief

experience on the road was sufficient to convince a majority
of the migrants that transiency did not provide a solution of
their problems. This conclusion helps to explain the fact that
the transient relief population did not increase in size with
anything like the rapidity that might have been expected during
the period of more than two years that transient camps and
shelters were operated in forty-seven of the States. Moreover,
three years of severe unemployment had passed before the Transient Program was established; and if all, or even a majority,
of those who set out during those years had remained on the
road, the transient population would have easily reached the
million or more that was anticipated at the time the Relief
Act of 1933 was passed. [1]

There remained, however, a minority of both the unattached
persons and family groups that, at the time of registration,
had been on the road for one year or more, a period of time
long enough to suggest that migration was becoming an end in
itself rather than a means of regaining stability. During the
seven-month period examined, 6 to 8 percent of the unattached
persons, and 8 to 10 percent of the family groups had been
migrants for one to two years; 3 to 5 percent of both groups,
for two to three years; and 2 percent of the family groups, and
2 to 3 percent of the unattached persons, for three to four
years.

It is probable that a large part, and possible that all, of
those who had been transients for one to four years would return to stability with the improvement of business conditions.
But most of those who had been on the road for four years or
longer would seem to be permanently a part of that group whose
lives are an endless series of migrations. Among the unattached
persons from 8 to 10 percent, and among the family groups 3 to
7 percent, had been on the road four years or longer. It is
known that this group was composed almost entirely of migratory
workers who were not properly a part of the depression migration
represented by the transient relief population.

Actually, the migratory worker was specifically excluded from
eligibility for relief under the Transient Relief Program, on
the grounds that relief for this group would represent a subsidy
to industries dependent upon a mobile labor supply. Only a few
of the States attempted to enforce this ruling for the simple
reason that unless the applicant admitted to being a migratory
worker there was no way of distinguishing him from the depression migrant. As it turned out, the ruling was unnecessary.
An examination of a considerable number of case histories shows
that only as a last resort did the migratory worker turn to
the transient bureaus for assistance. Out of years of experience

---

[1] See page 12.

he had learned how to live on the road, and he resented both
the necessity of asking for relief and the regulations that
were attendant upon its receipt. The migratory worker remained
throughout the depression a "rugged individualist" who objected
to any interference with his way of life.

Mobility of the Transient Relief Population

In the discussion of monthly rates of addition to the transient relief population it was noted that the rate varied
roughly, and in the same direction, with total registrations,
both in the thirteen cities and in the country as a whole.
However, a comparison of the rates of addition (see Table 25,
Appendix B) with total registrations (see Table 1; and Charts
I, II, and III) shows that monthly registrations were much more
variable than rates of addition. Although there is no question
that the variation in the monthly rate of addition did affect
the number of registrations,[1] there was another and more important factor responsible for the sharp rise in registration during
the spring and summer months, and the decline in fall and winter.
That factor was the variation in the mobility of the transient
relief population which resulted from changes in weather conditions and seasonal employment opportunities.

It is recognized that a discussion of mobility is, in effect,
a discussion of transiency. But a distinction does exist. For
purposes of relief, a transient was defined as a non-resident;[2]
and under the State settlement laws an individual becomes a
non-resident as the result of no more mobility than is involved
in a single move across a State boundary followed by a period
of stability insufficient to meet the legal residence require-
ment. On the other hand, all mobile non-residents, in the
sense of continued or repeated movements about the country,
became a part of the transient relief population as soon as

---

[1] At first thought this may seem too obvious to mention. But further consideration will show that changes in the mobility of those already in the
transient relief population could have offset variations in registration
caused by newcomers registering for the first time. For instance, if 20
percent of the population registered during any one month were newcomers,
and if during that month an equal number of transients already in the
population remained the entire month in one place so that they did not appear
in the registration figures for that month, no change would appear in the
number of registrations as a result of these additions to the population.
Of course, the same effect could have been caused by withdrawals, provided
that all those who withdrew did not register at any transient bureau during
the month; that is, if they withdrew from a place in which they had registered in a previous month. But in effect that likewise would amount to a
decline in mobility.

Actually, variations in monthly registrations were the net result of
changes both in the rate of addition and in mobility. At times these two
factors had the same, and at times, the opposite, effect on total registrations for the month.
[2] See page 11.

MODE OF TRAVEL

UNATTACHED

FAMILY GROUPS

OWN AUTOS

HITCH HIKED

PAID FARE

RODE RAILS

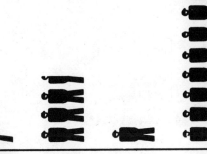

EACH BLACK FIGURE REPRESENTS 10,000 PERSONS

DIVISION OF SOCIAL RESEARCH AF-901

they applied for assistance.   Therefore, within the transient
relief population the range of mobility was from a single move
across State lines by an individual or family that had neither
the intention nor the desire of continuing migration, to the
continued wanderings of the chronic hobo and the migratory
worker. Between these extremes were all gradations of mobility; moreover, not only did mobility vary from individual to
individual, but with the same individual from month to month.

It is the purpose of the pages that follow to demonstrate
the changing mobility of the transient relief population (1)
in the country as a whole, and (2) in ten States selected to
represent different sections of the country. Use will be made
of the ratio of total registration, by months, to the mid-
monthly census of cases under care, to show changes in the
mobility of the transient relief population at different times
of the year.[1]

1. In the discussion of the size of the transient relief
population,[2] it was noted that monthly registrations in the
country as a whole described the seasonal variation, while the
mid-monthly census of cases under care described the trend in
the transient relief activities. In the former, there were
wide monthly variations, while the latter was singularly free
from such variations. (See Chart 1, Chapter I and Table 1, Appendix B). When total monthly registrations are expressed in
terms of the number of registrations for each 100 cases under
care on the 15th (or16th)[3] of the month, the results are as follows:

TABLE D.   MONTHLY REGISTRATIONS PER 100 CASES[A] UNDER CARE ON
THE FIFTEENTH (OR 16TH) OF EACH MONTH, TOTAL UNITED STATES

MONTH AND YEAR	REGISTRATIONS PER 100 CASES UNDER CARE	
	UNATTACHED PERSONS	FAMILY GROUPS
1934		
FEBRUARY	135	55
MARCH	170	55
APRIL	204	50
MAY	223	55
JUNE	233	58
JULY	265	53
AUGUST	282	58
SEPTEMBER	241	56
OCTOBER	227	57
NOVEMBER	185	49
DECEMBER	135	40
1935		
JANUARY	140	38
FEBRUARY	135	32
MARCH	182	35
APRIL	207	39

A   COMPUTED FROM DATA IN TABLE 1, APPENDIX B.

[1]This ratio will be expressed in terms of the total number of registrations
each month for each 100 cases under care on the fifteenth of the month.
Total registrations represented all cases that applied for, and were

In February 1934, the ratio of registrations of unattached persons to each 100 persons under care on the 15th of the month was 135. Thereafter, the ratio increased each month, until August, when it was 282, more than twice the February ratio. Following August, the ratio declined each month excepting January, until February 1935 when it was 136, almost exactly the ratio in February a year earlier, despite the fact that the transient relief population had more than doubled in size during the twelve months. From a low of 136 in February 1935, the ratio increased to 207 in April, in comparison with 204 in April a year earlier.

Since these ratios show the relationship of total monthly registrations of unattached persons to total cases under care on one day of each month, it seems obvious that the marked increase during the spring and summer months could not have been entirely the result of additions[1] to the transient relief population. Instead, the increase was, for the most part, the result of increased mobility both of those already in, and those who came into, the population during this period. The increase in mobility was principally a response to the obvious advantages

---

given relief at any time during the month. The mid-monthly census was a count of all persons who received care during a period of twenty-four hours on the fifteenth of the month. (See page 20 for further discussion of these two methods of reporting.)

The value of the ratio of registrations to cases under care as a measure of mobility comes from the fact that each registration (as distinguished from a case under care) necessarily involved a movement to the place of registration. If only one move was made, a single registration was reported, and the person was not registered again as long as he remained under care in that place. However, if the same person was en route, and stopped at transient bureaus along the way, he was reported in the monthly registration figures as many times as he received relief, either in the same State, or in different States.

The mid-monthly census of cases under care included all persons present on the day of the census, regardless of the length of time they had been under care. Thus, the person who had been in the bureau for six months was reported in six mid-monthly censuses, although he was included in the registration figures for only one of the months.

Therefore, neglecting additions and withdrawals, if the ratio of registrations to each 100 cases under care was 100, it meant that either the total transient population had moved once during the month, or that part of the population had moved more than once while the other part remained in one place. A ratio of less than 100 was evidence of a smaller number of movements or of those who moved; while a ratio of more than 100 was evidence of an increase in movements, or movers.
[2] See pages 18 to 22, particularly page 22, Chapter 1.
[3] When the 15th fell on Sunday, the census was taken on the Monday following. It is possible that the day on which the 15th or 16th fell may have had a slight effect on the number of persons under care, because of intra-weekly variations.
[1] As pointed out earlier (see page 65), the monthly rates of addition to the population during the months for which data were available varied in much the same manner as did registrations. Undoubtedly the increase in the rate of addition, and probably a decrease in the rate of withdrawals, helped to swell the number on the road during the period of favorable weather; but had this been the only factor, the number of cases under care should have risen almost as rapidly as did registrations, which, as just shown by the ratios, was not the case.

of traveling when the weather was mild; but it was also a response to the demands, or the possibility of demands, of seasonal industries for a mobile labor supply.

In marked contrast with the wide fluctuations in the mobility of unattached persons was the restricted mobility of family groups. In none of the sixteen months shown in Table D, (page 70) did total monthly registrations approach equality with the number of family groups under care on the fifteenth of the month. The ratios of monthly registrations to each 100 family groups under care varied from a maximum of 68 in August 1934, to a minimum of 32 in February 1935, in contrast with 282 and 136 respectively for unattached persons in these particular months. Using the ratios as rough indices of mobility, it may be said that unattached transients as a group were approximately four times as mobile as transient families.

It was noted earlier that monthly registrations were less variable from month to month,[1] and that the monthly rate of addition was lower[2] for family groups than for unattached persons. These findings taken in conjunction with the comparatively low ratios of monthly registrations to cases under care, seem to offer conclusive proof that the migration was much more difficult for family groups than for unattached persons.[3] As a result, transient families tended to remain under care in one place for considerably longer periods of time once they had become a part of the transient relief population[4] than did unattached persons.

Although restricted, the mobility of family groups was affected by seasonal factors in much the same manner as was the mobility of unattached persons. In February 1934, the ratio of family group registrations to each 100 families under care was 55. With the exception of April, the ratio increased steadily to 68 in August, and declined thereafter to 32 in February 1935. From the low point in February, the ratio rose again, to 39 in April. Weather conditions probably had an even more important effect on the movement of family groups than was the case with unattached persons. The inclusion of women and children in family groups made travel by "hitch-hiking" and family automobile—the principal means of travel used by family groups—extremely difficult during inclement weather. It

---

[1] See page 22.
[2] See pp. 64 and 65.
[3] It should also be noted that family groups were more likely to be transients in the sense of non-residents with little or no record of migration, than was true of unattached persons. See pp. 68 and 69.
[4] See Chart 1, Chapter 1; and Table 1, Appendix B, which show that the number of family groups under care on the fifteenth of each month increased steadily during fourteen of the sixteen months, and that the number under care on February 15, 1935, was more than three times the number on the same date a year earlier.

seems probable that the difficulties of migration offer the best explanation of the fact that, on a basis of cases under care, the number of family groups never totaled as much as one-quarter of the unattached cases under care in the same month, and on a basis of cases registered never totaled as much as one-thirteenth of the unattached cases registered during the same month.[1] (See Table 1, Appendix B.)

From this discussion of the mobility of unattached and family group transients, it seems apparent that transiency as a depression phenomenon was primarily the migration of unattached persons; and the reasons for this are not hard to find. Travel, for the unattached person, was relatively easy. The vast network of railroad communication carried him directly and rapidly into any section of the country. Shelter and food could be obtained much more readily by the unattached person than by the family group. Where transient bureaus were not available, the unattached person could turn to jails, missions, municipal lodging houses, and, at worst, the "jungles" for a night's shelter; food could usually be obtained by solicitation, or in exchange for a few hour's work, or as a result of "panhandling". In contrast, the family group, particularly when children or aged persons were included, was severely handicapped as to means and rapidity of travel, and in securing food and shelter while en route.

2. The mobility of unattached persons in individual States as indicated by the relationship of monthly registrations to cases under care varied with the location of the State and the season of the year. Chart VIII presents registrations and cases under care reported by ten States located in different sections of the country.[2] Registrations are shown by solid lines, and cases under care by dotted lines.

When the ratios of total monthly registrations to each 100 cases under care on the middle of the month are computed for

---

[1] Unfortunately, there has been a tendency to use the total number of *individuals* in transient family groups rather than the number of family *groups* in making comparisons between the number of unattached and family group transients. This has led to the impression that family groups represented 40 to 50 percent of the transient relief problem, which was true only on the basis of the total number of individuals receiving relief on one day each month. This view ignored the fact that among unattached transients the unit of movement and relief was the individual, while among transient families the unit of movement and relief was the group.

[2] The selection of the States was determined both by the desire to report different parts of the country, and by the fact that ten of the thirteen cities included in the Research Section's study of transients were located in these States.

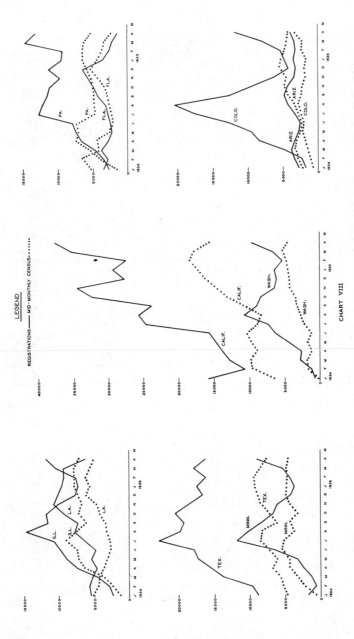

LEGEND

REGISTRATIONS ——— MID-MONTHLY CENSUS ······

CHART VIII

TRANSIENT REGISTRATIONS AND CASES UNDER CARE FOR SELECTED STATES

UNATTACHED TRANSIENTS

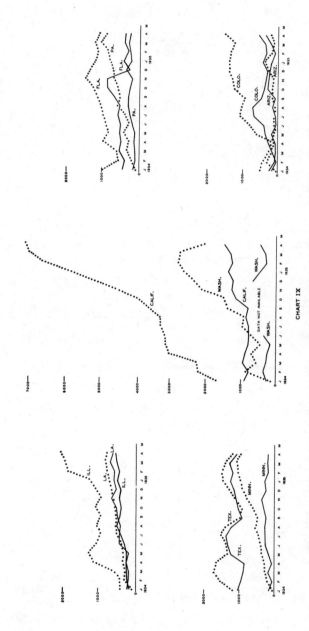

TRANSIENT REGISTRATIONS AND CASES UNDER CARE FOR SELECTED STATES

TRANSIENT FAMILY GROUPS

CHART IX

LEGEND

REGISTRATIONS —— MID-MONTHLY CENSUS······

these ten States at three-month intervals,[1] the results are as
follows:

TABLE E.   MONTHLY REGISTRATIONS OF UNATTACHED PERSONS PER 100 CASES UNDER CARE
ON THE FIFTEENTH (OR 16TH) OF THE MONTH, FOR SELECTED STATES AND MONTHS[A]

STATE	1934				1935
	FEBRUARY	MAY	AUGUST	NOVEMBER	FEBRUARY
ILLINOIS	104	121	163	151	99
LOUISIANA	127	164	213	223	153
TEXAS	190	272	243	222	193
MINNESOTA	29	78	273	118	96
WASHINGTON	65	237	357	173	117
CALIFORNIA	122	170	316	233	150
PENNSYLVANIA	88	98	239	170	148
FLORIDA	45	89	116	144	70
COLORADO	186	438	699	331	244
ARIZONA	108	110	152	72	69

A   DATA FROM REPORTS OF THE DIVISION OF TRANSIENT ACTIVITIES.

The mobility of unattached persons, as measured by the ratio
of monthly registrations to cases under care, was higher in
seven of the ten States during August, in two of the States
during November, and in one of the States during May, than during the other months for which ratios were computed. But for
all of the ten States excepting Arizona, mobility was lower
during February than during May, August, or November, 1934.
This suggests that low mobility during the winter months was a
common characteristic of the unattached transient population
in all parts of the country—a view that is confirmed by the
ratios for February, 1935.

The two States in which mobility was higher during November
than during the other months observed, were Florida and Louisiana.   This was partly the result of a movement of unattached
transients to these States for the purpose of avoiding the
rigorous northern winter, and partly the result of employment
possibilities in the winter resort centers. The State in which
mobility was higher in May was Texas, where the demand for
seasonal agricultural labor attracted the unattached transient.

The seven States in which mobility was higher during August
than during November, February, or May, are so located as to
permit the general conclusion that in most parts of the country mobility was determined primarily by weather conditions.
However, it must be noted that mobility varied widely even
among the seven States in which it was high during August.
For example, there were 699 unattached persons registered in
Colorado, and 152 in Arizona, for each 100 persons under care
on the fifteenth of the month.   The variation in mobility

---

[1]February, May, August, and November were chosen as the months best suited
to show the changing mobility in the ten States selected.

amoug the States was the result of a wide variety of circumstances, including the policy and the facilities of the State
Transient Relief Administrations, scenic attractions, employment opportunities, and the location of the State in reference
to main lines of travel.

An examination of family group registration and cases under
care on the fifteenth of each month reveals the interesting
fact that in seven of the ten States represented in Chart IX,
the number of family groups under care did not exceed two thousand cases a month, and in eight of the ten States, registrations did not exceed one thousand cases a month. Therefore, in
most of the ten States, the ratios of monthly registrations to
cases under care would be unreliable indices of family group
mobility, because of the small numbers involved.

However, it is possible to draw some inferences concerning
family group mobility from the curves in Chart IX. In three of
the ten States—Louisiana, Texas, and Arizona—the number of
registrations and cases under care was much the same during the
greater part of the sixteen months examined. This indicates
relatively high mobility (a ratio of approximately 100) for
family groups, and suggests that families in these States were
en route to such States as California, where mobility, as indicated by the steady increase in the number of cases under
care despite a fairly constant number of registrations, was very
low. In Illinois, the number of family groups under care varied
more than registrations, while in Washington, Florida, and
Colorado both registrations and cases under care varied considerably, at times in the same, and at times in opposite, direc-
tions. The accumulation of cases under care in California and
Washington, accompanied by a relatively small monthly registration, may be taken as an indication that these States were the
destinations of many of the family groups registered, and that
therefore mobility within these States was low. To a lesser
extent, this was true of Minnesota, Pennsylvania, and Colorado,
and perhaps also of Illinois.

The only general conclusion concerning the mobility of family groups that can be drawn from the data in Chart IX is that
family group mobility was low, in comparison with unattached
transients, and that it was lowest in those States which appear
to have been the objective of family group migration.

Origins and Destinations of the Transient Relief Population

There remain to be considered the origins and destinations
of the transient relief population. Origins will be presented
in terms of the State of residence before migration; and destinations, in terms of the net gain or loss that resulted from
the movements of the transient relief population. The data and

the discussion will be limited to those interstate (or Federal)
transients who were in some State other than the one from which
they began migration, on the date of each quarterly census. [1]

Origins

An examination of origins by geographic divisions discloses
the fact that at the end of each of the four quarters, the East
North Central Division (Ohio, Indiana, Illinois, Michigan, and
Wisconsin) ranked first as the origin of unattached transients;
while the West South Central Division (Arkansas, Louisiana,
Oklahoma, and Texas), ranked first as the origin of family
groups. (See Table 26, Appendix B; and Maps 1 and 2.) The East
North Central States were the origin of 19 to 21 percent of the
unattached persons, and the West South Central States, of 18 to
21 percent of the family groups.   The Middle Atlantic Division
(New York, New Jersey, and Pennsylvania) was next in importance
as the origin of unattached persons; while the West North Central Division (Minnesota, Iowa, Missouri, North Dakota, South
Dakota, Nebraska, and Kansas) was second in importance at three
of the quarterly censuses as the origin of family group transients.

The Mountain Division (Montana, Idaho, Wyoming, Colorado,
New Mexico, Arizona, Utah, and Nevada) was the least important
source of unattached transients, accounting for only 5 to 6
percent of the unattached transients at each quarterly census;
while the New England Division (Maine, New Hampshire, Vermont,
Massachusetts, Rhode Island, and Connecticut) was reported as
the origin of only 3 percent of the transient family groups.

When the proportions of transients coming from the several
Geographic Divisions are compared with the proportions of the
total population living in these Divisions, [2] there is provided
a rough index of the importance of the different sections of

---

[1] The state of origin of all transients under care in the United States on
the last day of each quarter was reported to the Division of Transient
Activities, beginning with the quarter ending September 30, 1934.   Data
for the last half of 1934 and the first half of 1935 will be used in this
discussion.   (See footnote 1, page 19).

The quarterly reports of origins do not distinguish interstate transients from intrastate and resident homeless persons, with the result
that States (e.g. Pennsylvania) which cared for any considerable number
of intrastate and resident homeless persons could not be compared ac-
curately with States that cared only for interstate transients.

In order to insure comparability for this discussion of origins and
destinations, a subtraction was made for each State of all persons whose
State of origin was the same as the State in which they were registered
for relief on the day the quarterly census was taken.

This procedure insures that only interstate transients are considered,
though it reduces their number slightly by eliminating the interstate
transient who happened to be passing through his State of origin and was
registered at a transient bureau in that State on the day of the census.

[2] Population of 1930, by Geographic Divisions.   See Fifteenth census, Vol.
1, Table 5.   These data are included in Table 26, Appendix B.

the country as sources of transiency. (See Table 26, Appendix
B.) The Census of 1930 shows that the Middle Atlantic Division
had the largest, and the East North Central Division, the
second largest, proportion of the total population. In comparison, the East North Central was more important than the
Middle Atlantic Division as a source of both unattached and
family group transients. The West North and West South Central Divisions ranked fourth and fifth respectively in the
proportion of the total population living in these Divisions
in 1930, but ranked second and first as the origin of transient family groups. Further comparison shows that the New
England States were under-represented and the Mountain States
over-represented in the transient population (both unattached
and family groups) in relation to the population in these areas
in 1930.

It is apparent from the data presented in the preceding
paragraphs that there was a significiant difference in the
origin of unattached and family group transients. This difference may be conveniently stated in terms of the proportions
of the two groups originating in the States East and West of
the·Mississippi River. (See Table F, below.)

TABLE F. PERCENTAGE OF UNATTACHED AND FAMILY GROUP TRANSIENTS ORIGINATING IN
STATES EAST AND WEST OF THE MISSISSIPPI RIVER

DATE OF CENSUS	EAST		WEST	
	UNATTACHED PERSONS	FAMILY GROUPS	UNATTACHED PERSONS	FAMILY GROUPS
1934				
SEPTEMBER 30	68	52	32	48
DECEMBER 31	64	48	36	52
1935				
MARCH 31	64	47	36	53
JUNE 30	64	45	36	55

At each of the four quarterly censuses a majority of the
unattached transients were from States east of the Mississippi
River, while this was true of family groups at only one census.
Moreover, the percentage of family groups from the States to
the east decreased from 52 percent on September 30, 1934, to
45 percent on June 30, 1935. Referring again to origins by
geographic divisions (see Table 26, Appendix B), it can be
seen that this difference between unattached and family group
transients follows from the fact that the two most important
sources of unattached transients were the East North Central
and Middle Atlantic Divisions, in contrast with the West North
and West South Central Divisions, for family groups. This suggests that unattached transients came most frequently from
States that were industrial rather than agricultural, whereas
the reverse was true of family groups.

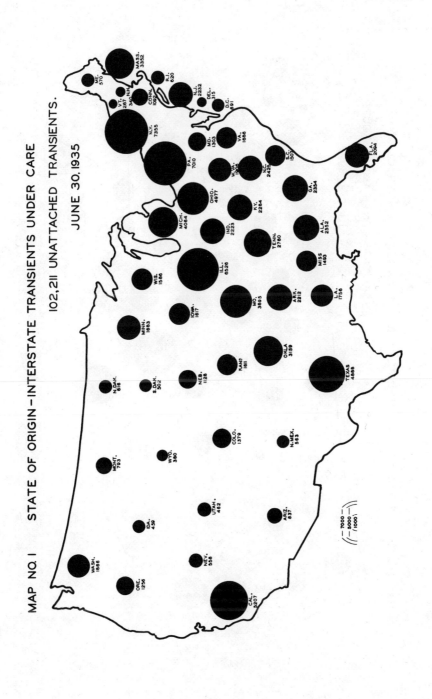

MAP NO.I   STATE OF ORIGIN-INTERSTATE TRANSIENTS UNDER CARE

102,211 UNATTACHED TRANSIENTS.

JUNE 30,1935

MASS.-
3352

ME.
570

N.H.
340

VT.
267

CONN.
1001

R.I.
620

N.J.
2232

DEL.
315

D.C.
691

N.Y.
7355

MD.
1303

VA.
1866

PA.
7010

W.VA.
1300

N.C.
2426

S.C.
1507

OHIO.
4977

GA.
2354

FLA.
2064

MICH.
4064

IND.
2223

KY.
2264

TENN.
2780

ALA.
2552

ILL.
6526

WIS.
1566

MISS
1493

MINN.-
1853

IOWA.
1617

MO.
3695

ARK.
2212

LA.
1756

N.DAK.
818

S.DAK.
502

NEB.
1128

KANS
1611

OKLA
3159

TEXAS
4886

MONT.
703

WYO.
360

COLO.
1379

N.MEX.
563

WASH.
1866

IDA.
450

UTAH.
462

NEV.
558

ARIZ.
837

ORE.
1256

CAL.
5207

7000
5000
1000

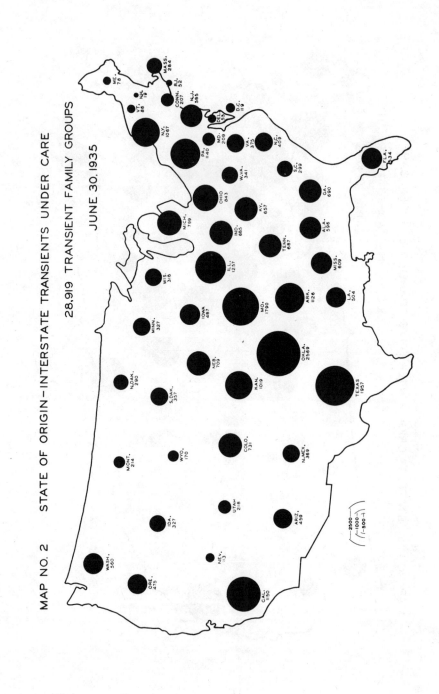

MAP NO. 2   STATE OF ORIGIN-INTERSTATE TRANSIENTS UNDER CARE

28,919 TRANSIENT FAMILY GROUPS

JUNE 30, 1935

ME. 75
VT. 86
N.H. 18
MASS. 264
CONN. 207
R.I. 52
N.J. 585
N.Y. 1067
D.C. 119
PA. 1140
DEL. 53
MD. 209
VA. 375
N.C. 409
OHIO 843
W.VA. 341
S.C. 299
MICH. 799
IND. 685
KY. 657
GA. 690
ILL. 1257
TENN. 687
ALA. 596
WIS. 318
MISS. 609
IOWA 487
MO. 1790
ARK. 1126
LA. 504
MINN. 327
NEB. 709
OKLA. 2569
N.DAK. 290
KAN. 1019
TEXAS 1957
S.DAK. 357
COLO. 731
MONT. 214
WYO. 170
N.MEX. 369
UTAH 218
ARIZ. 459
IDA. 327
NEV. 13
WASH. 560
ORE. 475
CAL. 1150
FLA. 234

2500
1000
500

When origins are considered by individual States, it is
found that New York, Pennsylvania, and Illinois were the States
most frequently reported by unattached transients; and that,
combined, these three States accounted for one-fifth of all
unattached transients at each of the four quarterly censuses.
(See Tables 27a and 27b, Appendix B.)   Each of these States
contributed as many unattached transients as did the nine
States of the Mountain Division, and approximately the same
number as the six New England States. The States most frequently
reported as the origin of transient family groups were Oklahoma, Texas, and Missouri.   These three States were reported
as the origin of 18 to 22 percent of the transient family
groups at each quarterly census; and each of the three contributed more family groups than did the six New England States.
In view of the frequent complaints of California citizens that
their State was being overrun by non-residents, it is interesting to note that California was included among the four or five
most important States of origin for unattached persons, and
among the three to six most important States of origin for family groups at each of the four quarterly censuses.

Migration from Rural and Urban Areas

The quarterly census of State of origin did not report the
number of unattached and family group transients coming from
rural and urban areas in each State. However, this information
is available for transients registered in the thirteen cities[1]
included in the Research Section's study for the period November
1934 through April 1935.   Rural is taken to mean farms, open
country, and towns with a population of less than 2,500 persons; and urban, to mean all towns and cities of 2,500 or more
persons, as reported by the Census of 1930.
Using this rough division of rural and urban, it can be said
that both the unattached and family group transients were predominantly urban in origin.[2] (See Table 28, Appendix B.) Dur-

---

[1] Interstate transients registered in the thirteen cities came from the
several States in much the same proportions as were found for the total
transient population under care in the United States at the end of each
quarter. The coefficient of correlation computed between the two distributions of origins by States, for December 1934, was .95 for both
unattached and family group transients, with a probable error of .01.
[2] The proportion of transients coming from urban centers was considerably
higher than the proportion of urban residents in the total population as
reported by the 1930 Census. If the total population of 1930 is classified
as urban and rural (using places of 2,500 population as the dividing line),
it is found that 56 percent were urban in contrast with approximately 80
percent of the unattached and 70 percent of the family group transients
included in this report.   In New York State 84 percent of the 1930 population was urban while slightly over 90 percent of the transients from
New York State came from urban centers.   In an agricultural State such as
Arkansas, the contrast is even more marked. The Census reports 21 percent
of the population as urban, while approximately 40 percent of the transients from Arkansas were urban.

ing each of the six months examined, approximately 80 percent of the unattached persons and 70 percent of the family groups came from places with 2,500 or more population. Among the transients that had lived in rural areas before migration, the proportion of families from farms and open country was only slightly higher, while the proportion from towns of less than 2,500 population was considerably higher, than the proportion of unattached transients.[1] Indeed, most of the difference in the proportion of the unattached and family group transients coming from rural areas is explained by the larger proportion of family groups from the small towns (under 2,500 population). The proportion of transients from farms and open country varied from 6.2 to 7.6 percent for unattached persons, and from 7.6 to 9.7 percent for family groups; while those from towns of less than 2,500 population varied from 12.6 to 13.9 for unattached persons and from 17.0 to 21.4 percent for family groups.

The definition of urban as all places with 2,500 or more population leaves unanswered the question of just how large these towns and cities were that contributed approximately 80 percent of the unattached persons and 70 percent of the family groups. To answer this question, urban origins of transients registered in the thirteen study cities were tabulated by certain customary size classifications for November and December, 1934, and March and April, 1935. The results are presented in Table 29, Appendix B.

In each of the four months examined, nearly half (46.0 to 47.9 percent) of the unattached persons came from cities of 100,000 or more population; between 6 and 7 percent, from cities of 50,000 to 100,000 population; an equal percentage from cities of 25,000 to 50,000; approximately 8 percent from cities of 10,000 to 25,000, and about 10 percent from cities of 2,500 to 10,000 population. Compared with the unattached, a smaller proportion of family groups came from cities of 100,000 or more population; about the same proportions from the three size classifications between 10,000 and 100,000; and a larger proportion from cities of 2,500 to 10,000.

These findings as to the urban and rural origins of transients indicate that large cities (100,000 or more population) were the most important source of unattached transients, while for family groups, smaller places (under 10,000 population)

---

[1] The tendency of rural residents to give the location of the nearest post office as their address was recognized in the Research Section's study, and special efforts were made to avoid this bias by questioning each non-farm registrant as to whether the residence was within or without the city or town limits of the place given as the last residence before migration.

were of about the same importance as large cities.   Farms and
open country outside the towns were the source of a relatively
small porportion of either group.

The small proportion of unattached transients from farms and
open country is a logical expectation in view of the large
number of unattached persons from such States as New York,
Pennsylvania, and Illinois, and from the East North Central and
Middle Atlantic States as a group.   It is a little surprising,
however, to find a relatively small porportion of family groups
from farms and open country in view of the number coming from
the West North and West South Central States as a group. It is
true that the proportion of families coming from urban centers
(2,500 or more population) in these States was smaller than the
proportion from urban centers in States east of the Mississippi
River.   But it is also true that the proportion of families
from small towns (under 2,500 population) in the West North and
West South Central Divisions was consistently larger than the
proportion from farms and open country.   In some months for
which information on urban and rural origins is available from
registrations in the thirteen cities, nearly half of the families from the Drought States (North Dakota, South Dakota, Nebraska, Kansas, Oklahoma, and Texas) in the West Central Divisions were from rural areas.   But even in these States the
proportions from small towns and villages exceeded the proportions from farms and open country.

Destination of the Transient Relief Population

Depression transiency differed from the more familiar types
of migration in this country in that it was a population movement which, more often than not, lacked a definite destination.
The better-known migrations in the United States have been the
movement of population to new land during the extension of the
frontier; and the shift of population from rural to urban areas
after the frontier had disappeared.   The participants in both
of these movements had fairly definite objectives;   and once
these objectives were reached, a period of settlement followed.
As a result it is possible to trace the effects of these migrations on the distribution of population.[1]

The lack of a definite destination and the relatively short
period of time for which observations are available,   make it
difficult to determine the effect that depression transiency
had on the relocation of population.   The origin of the transient relief population under care at each of four quarterly
censuses has already been shown; and from these census reports
it is a simple matter to determine the location of transients
on the day of the census. But since there is no assurance that

---

[1] See G. W. Thornthwaite, Internal Migration in the United States, Philadelphia, 1934.

the location of the transient relief population on the census
date represented more than a temporary break in their migration,
this information is an unsatisfactory indication of population
changes. However, when the location and the origin of the
transient relief population is reduced to a statement of net
gain or loss, by States, for each of the four quarterly censuses, it is evident that certain States consistently lost,
and others consistently gained, population.

The net gain or loss of each State has been computed from
the quarterly censuses of State of origin of transients under
care on the last day of each quarter during the last half of
1934 and the first half of 1935. Only interstate transients
were included in these computations,[1] which involved for each
quarterly census the subtraction of the total number of transients from each State that were under care in other States
(outflow) from the number of transients in that State from other
States (inflow). The results of these computations are shown
in a series of eight maps, numbered 3 to 10, inclusive; four
showing net gain or loss by States for unattached transients,
and the same number for transient family groups. The net gain
or loss of each State is shown by a circle of area proportionate
to the number resulting from the subtraction of outflow from
inflow; and the amount of gain or loss appears below each circle.
Net gains are indicated by solid black circles and by numbers
without a sign prefixed, and net losses, by stippled circles and
numbers prefixed by a minus sign. A uniform scale (base circle)
was used in preparing the four maps for unattached persons, and
a uniform, though different scale (base circle) was used in
preparing the four maps for family groups.[2]

Unattached Transients. The maps representing net change in
the movement of unattached transients show that the number of
States that had gained or lost population at the end of each
quarter varied from census to census; and that this variation
was more pronounced in the States west, than in those east, of
the Mississippi River.[3]

---

[1]See footnote 1, page 75. Data showing the State of origin of interstate
transients under care on September 30 and December 31, 1934, and on
March 31 and June 30, 1935, are to be found in Tables 27a and 27b,
Appendix B. Hereafter these censuses will be referred to by months, to
avoid undue repetition of the day of the month and year.
[2]The difference in the number of unattached and family group cases necessi-
tated a change of scale. Therefore, comparisons cannot be made between
the number of unattached and family group transients on a basis of the
area of the circles.
[3]The Mississippi River is used throughout this discussion as a convenient
east-west division of the country.

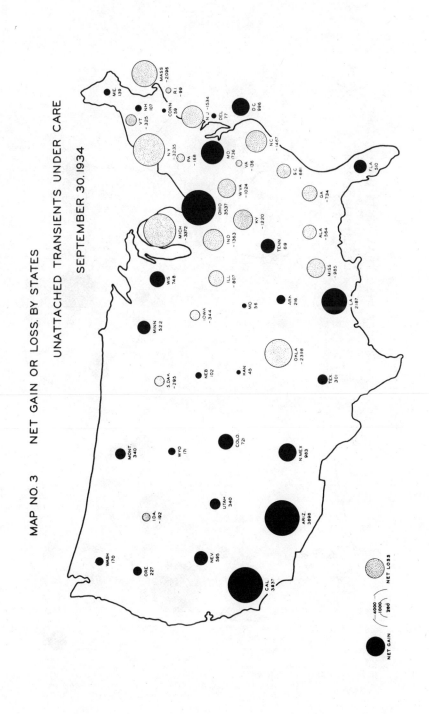

MAP NO. 3   NET GAIN OR LOSS. BY STATES

UNATTACHED TRANSIENTS UNDER CARE

SEPTEMBER 30. 1934

ME.
139

NH
107

MASS
-2096

RI
-99

VT
-325

CONN
59

N.J. -1534

DEL
77

D.C
996

N.Y
-3235

PA
-168

MD
1736

VA
-136

N.C.
-1467

FLA
510

OHIO
35537

W VA
-1024

S.C
-681

GA
-734

MICH
-3372

IND
-1363

KY
-1220

ALA
-564

TENN
619

WIS
748

ILL
-607

MISS
-985

LA
2187

MINN
522

IOWA
-344

MO
56

ARK
216

S.DAK
-295

NEB
102

KAN
45

OKLA
-2398

TEX
301

MONT.
340

WYO
171

COLO
721

N.MEX
983

IDA.
-192

UTAH
340

ARIZ.
3698

WASH
170

NEV
595

ORE
227

CAL
3037

NET LOSS

4000
1000
300

NET GAIN

MAP NO. 4   NET GAIN OR LOSS. BY STATES

UNATTACHED TRANSIENTS UNDER CARE

DECEMBER 31, 1934

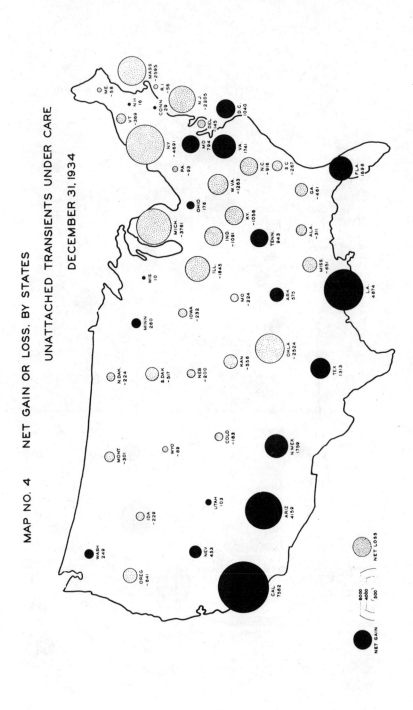

ME. -58
MASS -2595
N.H. 16
R.I. -56
CONN. 29
N.J. -2205
VT -369
N.Y. -4691
DEL. 145
D.C. 1040
PA. -93
MD. 794
VA. 1741
W.VA. -1263
N.C. -916
S.C. -207
MICH -3761
OHIO 176
KY. -1056
IND. -1091
TENN. 943
GA. -481
FLA. 1698
WIS. 10
ILL. -1845
ALA. -311
MISS. -651
MINN 260
IOWA -232
MO -224
ARK 575
LA 4874
N.DAK. -224
S.DAK. -517
NEB -200
KAN -556
OKLA -2524
TEX 1313
MONT -301
WYO -69
COLO -183
N.MEX 1759
IDA -229
UTAH 103
ARIZ 4159
WASH 249
NEV 453
OREG -641
CAL 7562

NET GAIN
NET LOSS
8000
3000
500

MAP NO. 5   NET GAIN OR LOSS, BY STATES

UNATTACHED TRANSIENTS UNDER CARE

MARCH 31, 1935

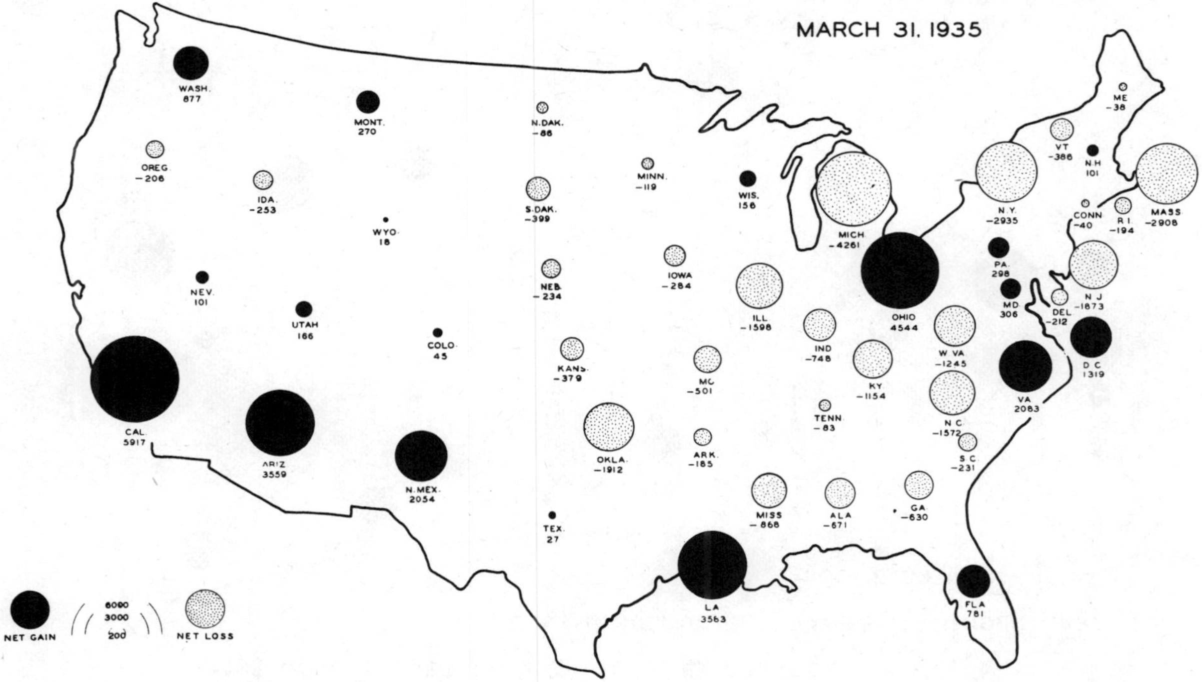

ME
-38

N.H.
101

VT
-386

MASS
-2906

R.I.
-194

CONN
-40

N.Y.
-2935

PA.
298

N.J.
-1873

DEL.
-212

MD.
306

D.C.
1319

VA.
2083

W.VA.
-1245

N.C.
-1572

S.C.
-231

GA.
-630

FLA.
781

OHIO
4544

MICH.
-4261

KY.
-1154

TENN.
-83

ALA.
-671

IND.
-748

ILL.
-1596

WIS.
156

MISS.
-868

LA.
3563

MINN.
-119

IOWA
-284

MO.
-501

ARK.
-185

OKLA.
-1912

TEX.
27

N.DAK.
-86

S.DAK.
-399

NEB.
-234

KANS.
-379

COLO.
45

N.MEX.
2054

WYO.
18

MONT.
270

UTAH
166

ARIZ.
3559

IDA.
-253

NEV.
101

WASH.
877

OREG.
-206

CAL.
5917

NET LOSS

6000
3000
200

NET GAIN

MAP NO. 6   NET GAIN OR LOSS, BY STATES

UNATTACHED TRANSIENTS UNDER CARE

JUNE 30, 1935

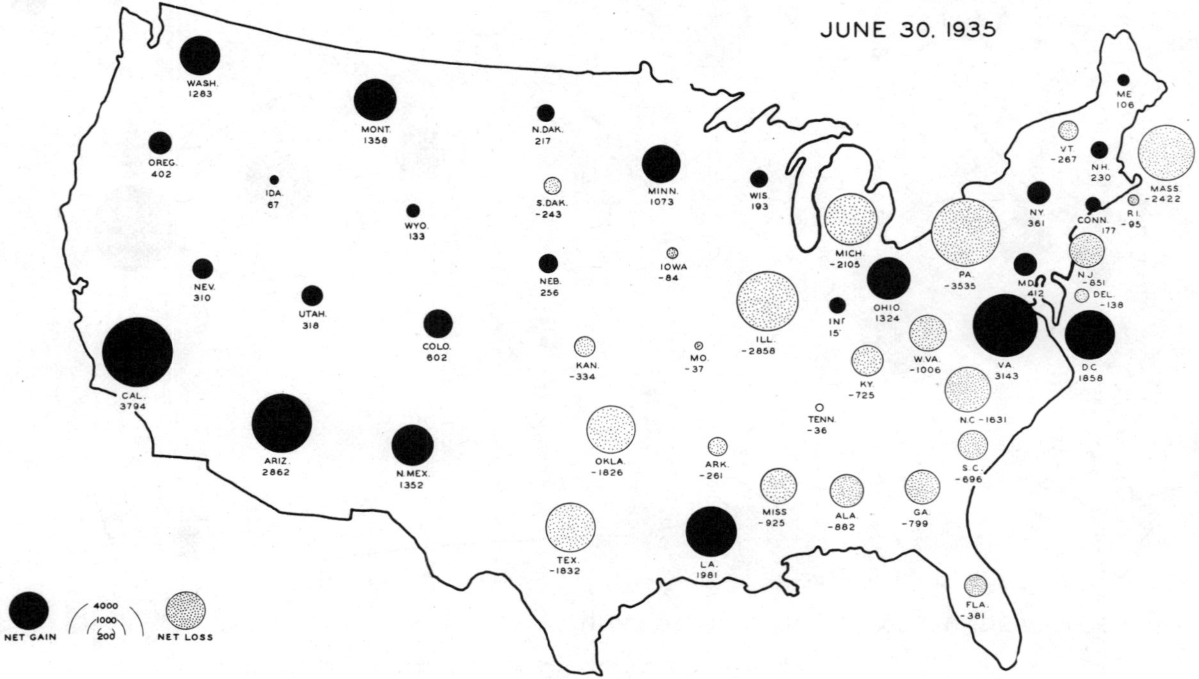

ME. 106
N.H. 230
VT. -267
MASS. -2422
R.I. -95
CONN. 77
N.Y. 361
N.J. -851
DEL. -136
MO. 412
D.C. 1658
PA. -3535
VA. 343
N.C. -1631
S.C. -696
FLA. -361
W.VA. -1006
OHIO 1324
IND. 15
KY. -725
GA. -799
MICH. -2105
ALA. -882
TENN. -36
WIS. 193
ILL. -2858
MISS. -925
MINN. 1073
IOWA -84
MO. -37
ARK. -261
LA. 1961
N.DAK. 217
S.DAK. -243
NEB. 256
KAN. -334
OKLA. -1826
TEX. -1832
COLO. 602
WYO. 133
N.MEX. 1352
MONT. 1358
UTAH. 318
ARIZ. 2862
IDA. 67
WASH. 1283
NEV. 310
CAL. 3794
OREG. 402

4000   1000   200
NET LOSS

NET GAIN

TABLE G. NUMBER OF STATES WITH NET GAINS OR LOSSES FROM THE MOVEMENT OF INTERSTATE
UNATTACHED TRANSIENTS, AT EACH OF FOUR QUARTERLY CENSUSES

CENSUS DATE	ALL STATES[A]		EAST OF MISSISSIPPI RIVER[B]		WEST OF MISSISSIPPI RIVER	
	NET GAIN	NET LOSS	NET GAIN	NET LOSS	NET GAIN	NET LOSS
1934						
SEPTEMBER 30	28	21	10	17	18	4
DECEMBER 31	19	30	9	18	10	12
1935						
MARCH 31	19	30	8	19	11	11
JUNE 30	25	24	10	17	15	7

A FORTY-EIGHT STATES AND THE DISTRICT OF COLUMBIA.
B TWENTY-SIX STATES AND THE DISTRICT OF COLUMBIA.

The number of States east of the Mississippi River with net gains or losses at each census remained fairly constant; while west of the Mississippi there was considerable variation. Furthermore, thirteen States east of the Mississippi had net losses, and five had net gains, at each of the four censuses. In contrast, only three States west of the Mississippi had net losses, and seven, net gains, at each of the censuses. In all, then, twenty-eight of the forty-eight States and the District of Columbia either gained or lost in exchange of unattached transients at each census; and the remaining twenty-one States had mixed gains and losses; that is, changed from gain to loss, or vice versa, at least once during the period examined. These findings may be conveniently arranged as follows:

States East of the Mississippi River

Net gain at each census	Net loss at each census	Mixed gains and losses
District of Columbia	Alabama	Connecticut
Maryland	Georgia	Delaware
New Hampshire	Illinois	Indiana
Ohio	Kentucky	Florida
Wisconsin	Massachusetts	Maine
	Michigan	New York
	Mississippi	Pennsylvania
	New Jersey	Tennessee
	North Carolina	Virginia
	Rhode Island	
	South Carolina	
	Vermont	
	West Virginia	

States West of the Mississippi River

Net gain at each census	Net loss at each census	Mixed gains and losses
Arizona	Iowa	Arkansas
California	Oklahoma	Colorado
Louisiana	South Dakota	Idaho
Nevada		Kansas
New Mexico		Minnesota
Utah		Missouri
Washington		Montana
		Nebraska
		North Dakota
		Oregon
		Texas
		Wyoming

Of the States with persistent net gains at each census, the more important were Ohio,[1] Maryland, and the District of Columbia, to the east of the Mississippi River; and California, Louisiana, Arizona, and New Mexico, to the west. The States with the more important and persistent net losses at each census were Michigan, Massachusetts, Illinois, North Carolina, New Jersey, and West Virginia, to the east, and Oklahoma, to the west, of the Mississippi River. Both the persistency and the size of the net gains or net losses are evidence that definite shifts in the unemployed population of these fourteen States resulted from the movement of unattached transients.

To these States in which population changes were clearly indicated, there should be added some of the States in which net gains and losses were mixed. But in view of the effect of seasonal factors on the movement of unattached transients,[2] and the fact that observations are available for only one year, it does not seem advisable to attempt more than tentative conclusions as to the nature of these changes. From the data available it seems probable that New York, Pennsylvania, Indiana, and Kansas lost, and that Minnesota, Virginia,[3] Florida, Tennessee, Montana, and Colorado gained in the exchange of unattached transients.

---

[1] It seems probable that the persistent net gain of Ohio was largely the result of a local migration from the adjoining States, particularly from Kentucky and West Virginia. In the discussion of inadequate relief as a reason for migration (See page 63), it was noted that when the standard of relief was actually, or reputedly, higher in óne State than another, the differential was an inducement to migration. Thus administrative factors frequently played a part in determining the destination of the transient relief population.
[2] See page 70.
[3] The gain in Virginia was solely the result of the establishment of a regional transient camp at Fort Eustis, which with three to four thousand transients under care was by far the largest camp in the country.

MAP NO. 7   NET GAIN OR LOSS. BY STATES

FAMILY TRANSIENT GROUPS UNDER CARE

SEPTEMBER 30. 1934

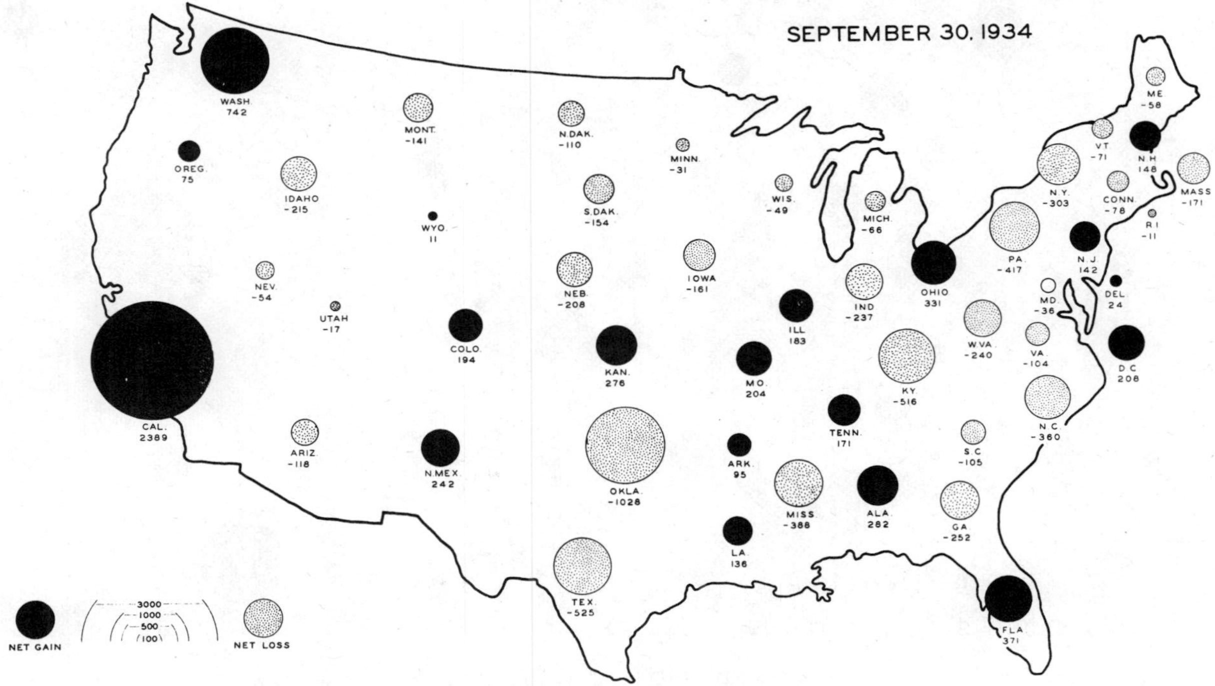

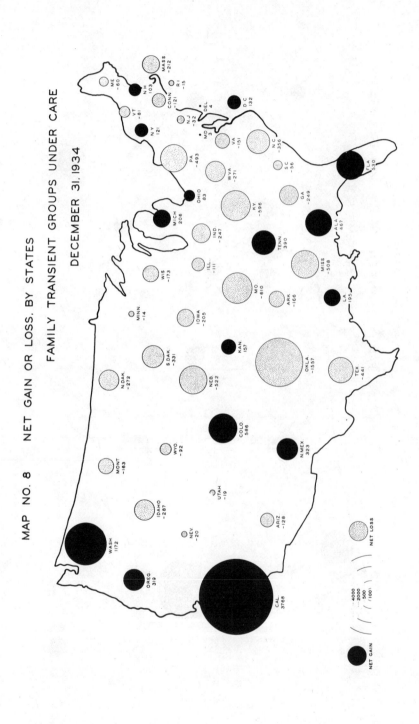

MAP NO. 8   NET GAIN OR LOSS, BY STATES

FAMILY TRANSIENT GROUPS UNDER CARE

DECEMBER 31, 1934

ME
-60

N.H.
103

VT
-81

MASS
-212

R.I
-15

CONN
-121

N.Y.
121

PA
-493

N.J.
-32

DEL
4

MD
3

D.C.
132

VA
-151

W.VA
-271

OHIO
83

MICH
206

IND
-247

ILL
-111

WIS
-173

KY
-596

N.C.
-356

S.C.
-56

GA
-249

FLA
530

TENN
390

ALA
467

MO
-610

ARK
-166

MISS
-508

LA
195

MINN
-14

IOWA
-205

KAN
157

OKLA
-1557

TEX
-441

S.DAK
-331

NEB
-522

N.DAK
-272

COLO
566

N.MEX
323

MONT
-163

WYO
-92

IDAHO
-287

UTAH
-19

NEV
-20

ARIZ
-128

WASH
1172

OREG
319

CAL
3768

NET LOSS

4000
2000
500
1000

NET GAIN

MAP NO 9   NET GAIN OR LOSS BY STATES

FAMILY TRANSIENT GROUPS UNDER CARE

MARCH 31,1935

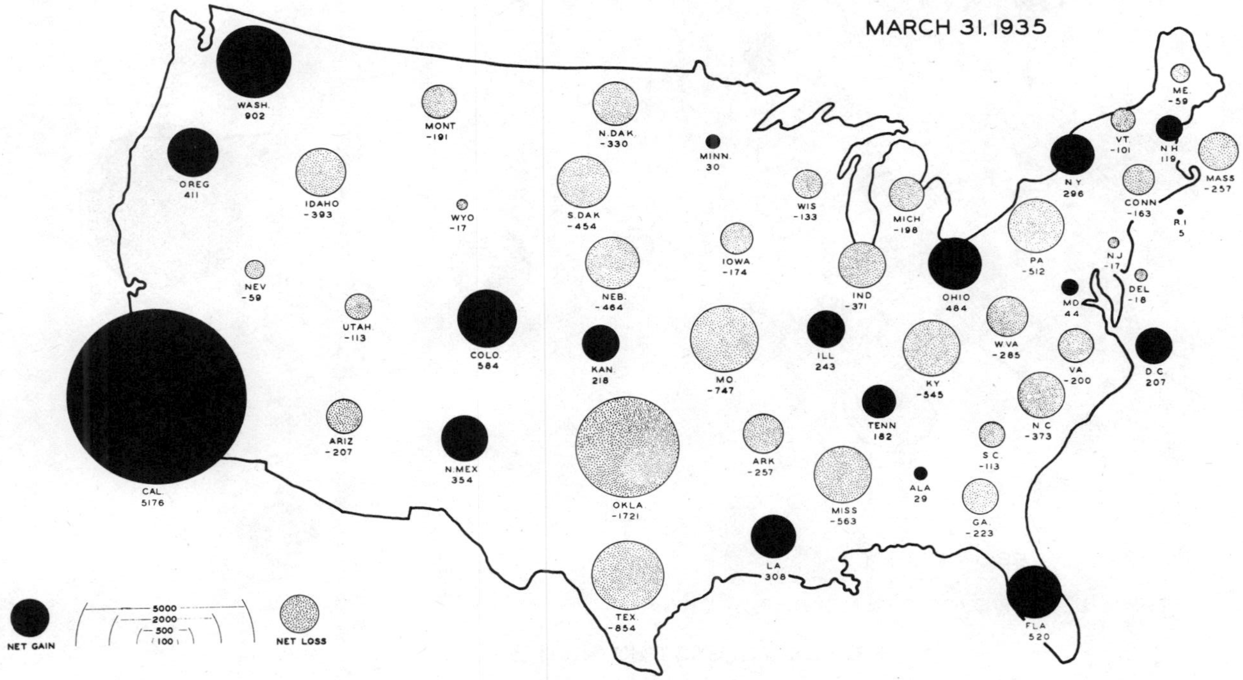

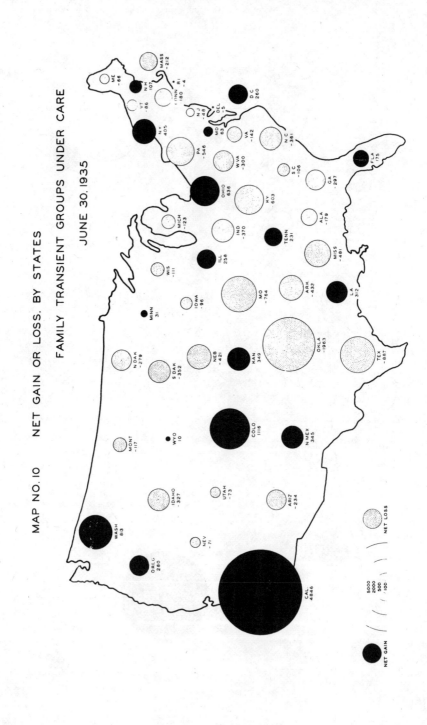

MAP NO. 10   NET GAIN OR LOSS, BY STATES

FAMILY TRANSIENT GROUPS UNDER CARE

JUNE 30, 1935

Combining the definite and the probable indications of population changes, it may be said that thirteen States gained, and eleven States lost unemployed persons through the movement of unattached transients. When these States are arranged in reference to the Mississippi River as an East-West dividing line, the results are as follows:

Population gains	Population losses
East of Mississippi River	
Ohio	Michigan
Maryland	Massachusetts
District of Columbia	Illinois
	North Carolina
Virginia	New Jersey
Florida	West Virginia
Tennessee	New York
	Pennsylvania
	Indiana
West of Mississippi River	
California	Oklahoma
Louisiana	Kansas
Arizona	
New Mexico	
Minnesota	
Montana	
Colorado	

These findings as to population changes show that unattached transiency was a movement out of the States in the Northern and Northeastern sections of the country, into the States in the Southern, Southwestern, and Western sections. The migration was principally into areas that were attractive by reasons of climate, topography, and repute; but areas that were unlikely to afford more than short-time seasonal employment.

Therefore, it seems possible to draw these general conclusions: The depression migration of unemployed (unattached) persons was away from the areas that, from the economic point of view, would be most likely to afford employment to them when industry recovered from the depression phase; that the redistribution of population resulting from unattached transiency was of a temporary nature; and that the greater part of this mobile unemployed group would return to urban-industrial areas as economic conditions improved.

Transient Family Groups. The number of States that had gained or lost population from the movement of transient family groups showed little variation from census to census. At the

end of the four quarters for which data are available, seventeen to nineteen States had net gains and thirty to thirty-two
had net losses.   The number of States east of the Mississippi
River that had net gains or net losses at each census was almost identical with the results shown in Table G, page 81, for
unattached transients; while west of the Mississippi, the variation in the number of States with net gains or losses was less
marked than for unattached persons.   A summary of the number
and location of States of net gain and loss at each census,
comparable to Table G for unattached persons, is presented below in Table H.

TABLE H.   NUMBER OF STATES WITH NET GAINS OR LOSSES FROM THE MOVEMENT OF INTERSTATE TRANSIENT
FAMILY GROUPS, AT EACH OF FOUR QUARTERLY CENSUSES

CENSUS DATE	ALL STATES[A]		EAST OF MISSISSIPPI RIVER[B]		WEST OF MISSISSIPPI RIVER	
	NET GAIN	NET LOSS	NET GAIN	NET LOSS	NET GAIN	NET LOSS
1934						
SEPTEMBER 30	19	30	9	18	10	12
DECEMBER 31	17	32	10	17	7	15
1935						
MARCH 31	18	31	10	17	8	14
JUNE 30	17	32	8	19	9	13

A FORTY—EIGHT STATES AND THE DISTRICT OF COLUMBIA.
B TWENTY—SIX STATES AND THE DISTRICT OF COLUMBIA.

The number, though not the identity, of States east of the
Mississippi River, that had persistent net losses, and net
gains, or mixed gains and losses at each of the four censuses
was practically the same for family groups as for unattached
persons.   West of the Mississippi, the number of States with
persistent net gains was the same, but, as shown by the comparison below, the number with persistent net losses, and with
mixed gains and losses was decidedly different:

	Net gains each census	Net losses each census	Mixed gains and losses
East of Mississippi River			
Family groups	5	14	8
Unattached persons	5	13	9
West of Mississippi River			
Family groups	7	11	4
Unattached persons	7	3	12

This comparison shows that the significant difference between family groups and unattached persons lies in the marked
increase in the number of States west of the Mississippi River
that had persistent net losses without at the same time reducing

the number of States with persistent net gains in the same section. This implies that an important part of the population
movement resulting from family group transiency was entirely
within the area west of the Mississippi River. The identity
and location of States with persistent net gains or losses,
and with mixed gains and losses, for family groups, are shown
below:

States East of Mississippi River

Net gain at each census	Net loss at each census	Mixed gains and losses
District of Columbia	Connecticut	Alabama
Florida	Georgia	Delaware
New Hampshire	Indiana	Illinois
Ohio	Kentucky	Maryland
Tennessee	Maine	Michigan
	Massachusetts	New Jersey
	Mississippi	New York
	North Carolina	Rhode Island
	Pennsylvania	
	South Carolina	
	Vermont	
	Virginia	
	West Virginia	
	Wisconsin	

States West of Mississippi River

California	Arizona	Arkansas
Colorado	Idaho	Minnesota
Kansas	Iowa	Missouri
Louisiana	Montana	Wyoming
New Mexico	Nebraska	
Oregon	Nevada	
Washington	North Dakota	
	Oklahoma	
	South Dakota	
	Texas	
	Utah	

A comparison of this with a similar classification for unattached persons (pp. 81–82) shows that of twelve States that had
persistent net gains for each group, seven (Ohio, New Hampshire
District of Columbia, California, Louisiana, New Mexico, and
Washington) were the same. In addition, the three States west
of the Mississippi River with a persistent net loss of unattached persons were included among the eleven States in that
area with a persistent net loss of family groups. Therefore,
it may be said that unattached and family group transients were

more nearly alike as to destinations than origins.

Among the States with a persistent net gain of family groups, California was easily the most important; and Washington, Colorado, Ohio, Florida, Oregon, New Mexico, and Louisiana followed, approximately in the order named. The States with the more important and persistent net losses at each census were Oklahoma, Texas, Kentucky, Pennsylvania, Mississippi, Nebraska, and South Dakota. Although both net gains and losses of family groups were smaller, they were more consistent than was true of unattached transients; that is, there were fewer States that changed from net gain to net loss, or vice versa, at one or more of the four quarterly censuses. This may be taken as additional evidence of the lower mobility of family groups in comparison with unattached persons, as well as the lesser effect of seasonal factors on their movements.[1]

In addition to the States with relatively large net gains or losses of family groups at each census, there were a number in which the gains or losses, though smaller, were of sufficient importance to warrant their inclusion among States in which definite population shifts occurred. On this basis, Kansas, Tennessee, and the District of Columbia should be added to the list of States that gained; and Massachusetts, North Dakota, Virginia, West Virginia, North Carolina, Georgia, Montana, Idaho, and Arizona, to the list of States that lost population. And finally, three of the States that had mixed gains and losses might be classified tentatively as having gained or lost population as a result of the migration of family groups. It seems probable that New York gained, and Arkansas lost, moderately; while the loss in Missouri was relatively large.

When the States with definite, and those with probable, indications of population changes are combined, it may be said that twelve States gained and eighteen States lost population as a result of family group migration. The identity and location of these States are presented below:

Population gains	Population losses
East of Mississippi River	
Ohio	Kentucky
Florida	Pennsylvania
New York	Mississippi
Tennessee	Massachusetts
District of	Virginia
Columbia	West Virginia
	North Carolina
	Georgia

---

[1] See pages 65 and 74.

Population gains	Population losses
West of Mississippi River	
California	Oklahoma
Washington	Texas
Colorado	Nebraska
Oregon	North Dakota
New Mexico	South Dakota
Louisiana	Missouri
Kansas	Arkansas
	Montana
	Idaho
	Arizona

This analysis of family group migration shows that the more important movement was away from States in the West Central section of the country, and particularly from the States in the Drought Area, to the States on the Pacific Coast. But there is also a fairly clear indication that east of the Mississippi River there were conflicting movements of families North and South, and perhaps, East and West.

West of the Mississippi River, the movement to the Pacific Coast States suggests a migration for the purpose of permanent relocation; while the gains of Colorado and Kansas suggest both the concentration of families moving out of the Drought Area, and the slow movement towards the Pacific Coast. Out of the conflicting movements east of the Mississippi River, Florida, because of its climate, gained population from the States along the Atlantic Coastline; and Tennessee gained population from the adjoining States as a result of the Tennessee Valley development. Otherwise the movement was out of the Southern States, and suggests a search for work, or higher relief standards. One evidence of this movement was the persistent net gains of Ohio and the District of Columbia. The net gain in New York State suggests a movement in response to a real or imagined differential in relief standards.

These findings point to the general conclusion that family group migration resulted in more definite population changes west, than east, of the Mississippi River. However, the lower mobility of family groups, the difficulties of travel, and the tendency of States to accept responsibility for non-resident relief families after a stay of one year, are valid reasons for believing that, in both areas, family group migrations resulted in more permanent shifts in the population than was true of unattached persons.

Chapter V

SUMMARY AND CONCLUSIONS

Summary

The transient relief population consisted of unattached individuals and family groups who were not legal residents of the community in which they applied for relief. Because non-residents were ineligible for relief from existing public agencies, special provision for their care was included in the Federal Emergency Relief Act of May, 1933. In the administration of relief under this provision, transients were defined as unattached persons or family groups that had not resided for one continuous year or longer within the boundaries of the State at the time of application for relief.

Early in the depression there were indications of an increase in the number of needy non-residents. During the fall and winter of 1930, municipal lodging houses, missions, and shelters in metropolitan areas reported that, in comparison with previous years, the number of homeless men seeking assistance was increasing rapidly. At about the same time, States in the South and West became alarmed at the influx of needy non-residents.

Because these depression migrants were constantly on the move, it was impossible to determine the number of different individuals included. During the Congressional hearings on relief legislation, the number of transients was estimated to be between one and one-half and five million persons. These estimates proved to be greatly in excess of the number of transients who received care under the Transient Relief Program.

The overestimates of the transient population were largely the result of applying the term "transient" to all homeless persons without reference to whether or not they had legal settlement; and the estimation of the total transient population from observations in areas where transients were most numerous. The Relief Act of 1933 did not refer to transients as such, but to "needy persons who have no legal settlement". When the Federal Emergency Relief Administration defined legal settlement as residence for twelve consecutive months in a State. it excluded the resident homeless of the large cities, who had been considered a part of the non-resident, or transient, population.

Even after the inauguration of the Transient Relief Program, it was impossible to determine with any degree of accuracy the size of this relief group. Actually, the transient population was not a definite and fixed group in the total relief population, but one that changed its membership constantly and was never the same on any two days in any one place. Based upon total monthly registrations for relief, the transient relief population reached a peak in August 1934 of 395,000 unattached persons and 16,000 family groups. But based upon the number of persons receiving care on one full day each month, the high

88

point was 176,000 unattached persons on January 15, 1935, and
40,000 family groups on February 15, 1935.

Total monthly registrations included duplications resulting
from the rapid movement of part of the population; while the
number under care on one full day a month did not include those
en route.   Therefore, the size of the population during any
month was somewhere between the number registered during the
month and the number under care on one day during that month.
Careful estimates place the maximum size during the operation
of the Transient Relief Program at 200,000 unattached persons
and 50,000 family groups.   But because the transient relief
population was constantly undergoing a change of membership,
it seems probable that the number of individuals and family
groups that *at some time* received assistance from transient
bureaus was two to three times these estimates.

The personal characteristics of the mobile relief population
were determined from registrations in thirteen cities, selected
to represent the several sections of the country.[1] During a
period of twelve months (May 1934 to April 1935), approximately two-thirds of the unattached persons and one-half of
the heads of family groups registered for relief in these
cities were between the ages of sixteen and thirty-five years.
The median age of unattached persons was between twenty-five
and thirty years; and the median age of family heads was between
thirty-three and thirty-five years.

Very few unattached women were included in the transient
relief population. Throughout the same twelve-month period for
which age data were obtained, the proportion of unattached women was less than 3 percent each month.   However, women were
frequently the heads of transient family groups; and when all
members of family groups (head and others) were considered, it
was found that females slightly outnumbered males in these
groups.

The great majority of transients were native white persons.
The proportion of Negroes among unattached transients (7 to 12
percent) was higher each month than among heads of family
groups (4 to 6 percent). Foreign-born whites did not exceed 5
percent of the unattached persons, nor 8 percent of the heads
of family groups in any of nine months for which registrations
were examined; Oriental and other color and nativity groups
represented only a very small proportion of either unattached
or family group transients.

---

[1] Most of the data presented in this summary were obtained from a special
study of transients registered in thirteen cities. To avoid undue repetition, reference to the thirteen cities has frequently been omitted in this
summary. This study was made by the Research Section, Division of Research,
Statistics, and Finance, Federal Emergency Relief Administration.

Approximately 80 percent of the unattached persons registered throughout a period of six months reported that they were
single; 10 percent, widowed or divorced; 4 percent, separated;
and 6 percent, married.   Among the heads of family groups, 84
to 88 percent reported themselves as married;   approximately 7
percent, widowed or divorced; 6 percent, separated; and 1 to 2
percent, as single.

Measured in terms of school years completed, transients were
fairly well educated. Only 2 percent of the unattached persons
and 3 percent of the heads of family groups had no formal education, and approximately two-thirds of both groups had a grade-
school education, or better.   Native white transients ranked
first in years of schooling completed; foreign-born whites,
second; Negroes, third; and other color and nativity groups,
last.

The average transient relief family was smaller by about
one person than the average family group in the general relief
population.   During a period of eight months (September 1934
through April 1935), the average size of transient families
was between 3.0 and 3.2 persons; while the average size of families reported by the Unemployment Relief Census of October,
1933, was 4.4 persons.

Over a period of seven months, 95 percent of the unattached
persons and 90 percent of the heads of family groups were employable in terms of physical ability and expressed willingness
to work at the time of registration for relief.   The principal
reasons reported for those unable to do gainful work were temporary and permanent disabilities, old age, and, among women
heads of family groups, the care of the family. Broad groupings
of usual occupations show that the proportion of unskilled and
semi-skilled workers in the transient relief population was
higher than the proportion of such workers in the general population.

Somewhat over half of the unattached persons and heads of
family groups reported that the duration of the last employment
at their usual occupation before migration was eighteen months
or longer. In contrast, over half of the jobs secured by transients during migration lasted less than two months; and nearly
one-quarter, less than fifteen days. Moreover, only about one-
third of the unattached persons and two-fifths of the heads of
family groups found any non-relief employment during their
wanderings. When the nature of this employment is examined, it
is found that a considerable proportion consisted of seasonal
and casual pursuits.

The most frequent reason for the depression migration of
needy persons and family groups was unemployment. Other reasons
of importance in the formation of the transient relief population were ill health, search for adventure, domestic trouble,

and inadequate relief.   It was seldom, however, that a single
reason provided an adequate explanation of the presence of the
individual or family group on the road. Therefore, a statistical statement of reasons for migration is used in this report
to indicate the order of importance among the principal reasons,
and brief summaries of typical cases, to describe the contingent
circumstances.

The examination of reasons for migration shows that depression transiency was not a simultaneous mass-migration in response to a single cause or group of causes.   Instead, the
transient relief population was constantly receiving additions
from the resident population. During any one month, the transient population was composed of persons who had been on the
road for varying periods of time. Over a period of seven
months, 15 to 21 percent of the unattached persons, and 11 to
16 percent of the family groups had begun migration during the
same month in which they registered for relief. During part of
this period, the transient population was declining in both the
thirteen cities and the total United States.   Therefore, it is
apparent that at times withdrawals from the transient population must have been equal to, or in excess of, additions.

Further evidence that the transient relief population was
constantly changing membership, and that its size was checked
by withdrawals, appears in the proportion of transients that
had been on the road for a period of six months or less. During
each of the seven months examined, roughly one-half to three-
fifths of the unattached persons and family groups had begun
migration within the six months preceding and including the
month of registration. If there had been no withdrawals
during this period, the size of the transient population and
the proportion that had been on the road for more than six
months, would have increased rapidly, which was not the case.

Total (United States) monthly registrations varied much
more than did the number of transients under care on one day
each month. Although some of the variations were caused by
changes in the rate at which newcomers were added to the population, the more important cause was the change in the mobility
of those already in the population. Mobility was relatively
low during the late fall and the greater part of the winter
months. Beginning in the early spring, there was a marked increase in mobility that continued until the end of August.
Thereafter, mobility decreased until the end of February. Unattached transients were much more mobile than transient families; but the mobility of both groups was unmistakably influenced by seasonal factors.   The seasonal increase in mobility
was principally a response to the obvious advantages of traveling when the weather was mild; but it was also a response to
the demands, or possibility of demands, of seasonal industries
for a mobile labor supply.

When the origins of the transient relief population (total United States) are considered, it is found that unattached transients came principally from the States to the east, and transient families from States to the west, of the Mississippi River. The East North Central Division (Ohio, Indiana, Michigan, and Wisconsin) ranked first as the origin of unattached transients; while the West South Central Division (Arkansas, Louisiana, Oklahoma, and Texas) ranked first as the origin of transient families. The proportion of transients coming from the several sections of the country did not correspond exactly with the proportion of the total population living in these sections as reported by the Federal Census of 1930. However, the lack of correspondence was greater for family, than for unattached, transients.

The proportion of transients coming from rural and urban areas could be determined only for registrants in the thirteen cities included in the Research Section's study. During a period of six months, approximately 80 percent of the unattached persons and 70 percent of the family groups came from places with 2,500 or more population. Furthermore, transients from rural areas came more frequently from small towns (under 2,500 population) than from farms and open country.

More often than not, transients lacked a definite destination, and their movements were determined to a large extent by climate, curiosity, and rumor. There was no assurance that the location of the transient relief population as reported by one-day quarterly census (total United States) represented more than a temporary break in their migration. However, when the location and the origin of the population was reduced to a statement of net gain or loss, by States, for each of four quarterly censuses, it was evident that certain States consistently lost, and others consistently gained, population.

Thirteen States east of the Mississippi River showed a net loss of unattached transients at each of the four quarterly censuses, while four States and the District of Columbia showed net gains. Only three States west of the Mississippi had net losses, and seven, net gains, at each census. In all, twenty-eight of the forty-eight States and the District of Columbia either gained or lost in exchange of unattached transients at each of the censuses; and the remaining twenty-one States changed from gain to loss, or vice versa, at least once during the period examined.

Of the States with persistent net gains of unattached transients the more important were Ohio, Maryland, and the District of Columbia, to the east of the Mississippi River; and California, Louisiana, Arizona, and New Mexico, to the west. The States with the more important net losses of unattached transients at each census were Michigan, Massachusetts, Illinois,

North Carolina, New Jersey, and West Virginia, to the east, and
Oklahoma, to the west, of the Mississippi River.

The number of States east of the Mississippi River that had
persistent net losses, and net gains, or net gains and losses,
at each of the four censuses was practically the same for family groups as for unattached persons. West of the Mississippi,
the number of States with persistent net losses, and with mixed
gains and losses was decidedly different. Eleven States west
of the Mississippi had persistent net losses of families, and
only four had mixed gains and losses. In comparison, only three
States west of the Mississippi had consistent net losses, and
twelve had mixed gains and losses of unattached transients.

Among the States with persistent net gains of family groups,
California was easily the most important; and Washington,
Colorado, Ohio, Florida, Oregon, New Mexico, and Louisiana
followed, approximately in the order named. The States with
the more important and persistent net losses at each census
were Oklahoma, Texas, Kentucky, Pennsylvania, Mississippi,
Nebraska, and North Dakota. Although both net gains and losses
of family groups were smaller, they were more consistent than
was true of unattached transients; that is, there were fewer
States that changed from net gain to net loss, or vice versa,
at one or more of the four quarterly censuses.

Conclusions

Some of the conclusions of this study of the transient relief population have been presented in connection with the de-
scriptive data of the preceding chapters. Others, that depend
upon the study as a whole, have been reserved until a summary
of the more important findings has been presented. It is believed that this report contains sufficient justification for
the general conclusions which follow.

The transient population was the result of two circumstances—widespread unemployment and population mobility. The
relief problem presented by this group was the result of a third
factor—legal settlement (or residence) as a prerequisite for
relief from public and private agencies in each community.
Population mobility is so familiar a circumstance in this country as to be considered a characteristic; and unemployment becomes a problem during each economic depression. It was the
conjunction of these two circumstances that formed the transient population and invoked the third factor. Because communities have always considered the claims of their unemployed
residents as superior to those of non-residents, the transient
population became an unwanted and excluded group in the general
unemployed population.

Except for the fact that they were non-residents, there seems little reason for considering transients as a distinct and separate group. Although they could be distinguished from the resident unemployed, it was principally because they were younger, and included a greater proportion of unattached persons. Actually the transient population represented the more active and restless element among the great number of unemployed created by the depression. Migration offered an escape from inactivity; and in addition, there was the possibility that all communities were not equally affected by unemployment.

The evidence in this report points to the conclusion that migration was an unsatisfactory solution of the problems that faced the unemployed during a depression period. Although nearly half of the transients studied found some employment during migration, most of this employment was of short duration. Moreover, the high mobility of the population was evidence that the transient found communities very much alike so far as the possibility of resettlement was concerned.

This depression migration lacked a definite destination, and thereby differed from the more familiar types of population movement. During the decade prior to the depression, the trend in population movement was from rural to urban areas. In contrast, the transient relief population was predominantly urban in origin, and these migrants traveled from city to city. This highly urban population was in search of cities that were less affected by the depression than the ones they had left; and, as a result, their movements were governed largely by rumor and curiosity.

Despite the aimless cross-currents of their movements, the transient population displayed a tendency to come more frequently from certain areas, and to go more frequently to others. There was a tendency for States east of the Mississippi River to lose more transients than they gained, although this was more clearly evident in the movement of unattached transients than of family groups. The compensating tendency was for States in the West and Southwest to gain more transients than they lost. Urban centers in Massachusetts, New Jersey, Illinois, and Michigan lost unattached transients to urban centers in New Mexico, Arizona, and California. The more important movement of family groups was from the towns and cities of the States immediately west of the Mississippi River to urban centers of California, Oregon, and Washington.

It seems apparent that a migration which resulted in an addition to the urban population of New Mexico, Arizona, Oregon, Washington, and even of California, must leave serious problems of assimilation, particularly when the migrants were without resources. The same may be said of the persistent gains of un-attached transients in Louisiana, and of family groups in Tennessee and Florida.

The migration of a considerable part of the transient relief population appears to have been a waste of effort. Much of the movement was away from urban areas that from the point of view of economic development were more likely to afford employment than were the areas which particularly attracted the transient. As business and industry recover, it may be expected that many of the depression transients will return to areas similar to the ones they left.

It seems evident from this study that the problem of depression transiency can be solved only through an adjustment of this mobile labor supply to areas where there is a demand for their services. Resettlement and stability are contingent upon economic opportunity.

The argument that the solution of the transient problem can be accomplished by an immediate return of all needy non-residents to their place of settlement appears to confuse the legal with the economic aspects of relief. Moreover, it has been shown[1] that of a representative sample of the transient relief population only slightly over one-half had verifiable legal settlement in a specific community. But aside from this obvious difficulty, there seems to be little logic in attempting to facilitate the return of transients to places of previous residence until, and unless, there is an opportunity for them to resume gainful employment.

Therefore, it seems highly probable that the dissolution of the transient population will proceed only as rapidly as business and industry can provide the employment essential to stability. To whatever extent this provision falls short, the transient problem will remain unsolved.

---

[1] See Legal Settlement Status and Residence History of Transients, Research Bulletin TR-9, Federal Emergency Relief Administration, Washington, D.C., August 30, 1935.

APPENDIX A

Bills and Hearings Concerning
Transient Relief

A careful examination of the relief bills introduced in the Congress from December 2, 1929, until March 4, 1933, shows that there were twelve bills which contained some provision for relief to needy non-residents. These bills are listed below in chronological order. The letters "H.R." and "S." before the bill numbers refer to the House of Representatives and the Senate, respectively. No record could be found of public hearings on six of these bills. The dates of the hearings on the others are listed under the appropriate headings. Copies of these bills and the hearings, when held, were printed by the Government Printing Office, Washington, D. C.

This information was compiled by the Research Library, Federal Emergency Relief Administration.

Number	Title	Committee	Author	Date of Introduction	Hearings
S. 174	To provide for cooperation by the Federal Government with the several States in relieving the hardship and suffering caused by unemployment, and for other purposes.	Commerce discharged and referred to Manufactures Dec. 17	Costigan	December 9, 1931	December 28,29,30, 1931; January 4-9, 1932
S. 262	To provide for assisting the several States and their political subdivisions in meeting the expense of emergency relief activities and to provide for the relief of the unemployed.	Manufactures	La Follette	December 9, 1931	December 28,29,30, 1931; January 4-9, 1932

Number	Title	Committee	Author	Date of Intro- duction	Hearing
H.R. 6716	To provide relief for unemployed itinerant workers having no perma- nent residence.	Labor	La Guardia	January 4, 1932	No record
H.R. 8088	To provide for cooperation by the Federal Government with the several States in re- lieving the hardship and suffering caused by unemployment, and for other purposes.	Labor	Lewis	January 20, 1932	February 1-5, 10, 11, 12, 1932
H.R. 8988	For relief of unemployed.	Labor	Lovette	February 8, 1932	No record
S. 3670	To authorize ap- propriations for the construc- tion of rural post roads in the several States for the purpose of fur- nishing employ- ment and there- by relieving the hardship and suffering caused by the existing depression, and to provide for cooperation by the Federal Government with the several States in reliev- ing the hardship and suffering caused by unem- ployment, and for other purposes.	Post Offices and Post Roads	Black and Bulkley	February 16, 1932	No record

Number	Title	Committee	Author	Date of Introduction	Hearings
H.R. 11926	To provide for cooperation by the Federal Government with the several States in assisting persons, including veterans of the World War, who are suffering from hardship caused by unemployment, and for other purposes.	Ways and Means	Lewis	May 6, 1932	No record
H.R. 4592	To provide for cooperation by the Federal Government with the several States in assisting persons, including veterans of the World War, who are suffering hardship caused by unemployment, and for other purposes.	Manufactures	Costigan	May 6, 1932	May 9, 1932; June 4, 1932
S. 5121	To amend title I of the Emergency Relief and Construction Act of 1932, approved July 21, 1932, by authorizing cooperation by Federal Government with the several States and Territories in relieving distress among unemployed needy transients.	Manufactures	Cutting	December 8, 1932	January 13 to 25, 1933

Number	Title	Committe	Author	Date of Introduction	Hearings
S. 5125	To amend the Emergency Relief and Construction Act of 1932.	Manufactures	Costigan and La Follette	December 8, 1932	January 3-17; February 2, 3, 1933
H.R. 13995	To provide for cooperation by the Federal Government with the several States in relieving the hardship and suffering caused by unemployment, and for other purposes.	Ways and Means	Lewis	January 3, 1933	No record
S. 5363	To provide for housing, feeding, and clothing of certain unemployed persons at Military posts of the United States.	Military Affairs	Couzens	January 10, 1933	No record

APPENDIX B

Supplementary Tables

TABLE 1.   TRANSIENT RELIEF REGISTRATIONS AND MID-MONTHLY CENSUS, TOTAL UNITED STATES[A]
AND REGISTRATIONS IN 13 SELECTED CITIES

YEAR AND MONTH	UNITED STATES TOTAL				13 CITIES TOTAL REGISTRATIONS	
	UNATTACHED PERSONS		FAMILY GROUPS			
	REGISTRATIONS	MID-MONTHLY CENSUS	REGISTRATIONS	MID-MONTHLY CENSUS	UNATTACHED PERSONS	FAMILY GROUPS
1934						
JANUARY	108,414	(B)	8,036	(B)	(C)	(C)
FEBRUARY	106,606	78,801	7,300	13,303	(C)	(C)
MARCH	154,121	90,502	8,196	14,791	(C)	(C)
APRIL	206,367	101,219	8,597	17,162	(C)	(C)
MAY	236,211	105,623	10,315	18,515	20,233	1,641
JUNE	267,378	114,848	11,715	20,142	22,590	1,827
JULY	342,414	122,346	13,979	22,149	25,152	2,048
AUGUST	395,384	140,156	16,232	23,822	29,090	2,277
SEPTEMBER	343,728	142,497	14,931	26,877	26,898	2,122
OCTOBER	343,032	151,006	15,997	28,703	25,160	1,908
NOVEMBER	310,533	167,264	15,926	32,760	23,412	2,064
DECEMBER	247,135	177,798	14,534	36,106	21,835	2,137
1935						
JANUARY	247,207	176,275	14,644	38,651	20,613	2,261
FEBRUARY	236,976	173,861	12,703	40,259	19,008	1,669
MARCH	315,118	173,471	14,220	40,125	23,953	1,759
APRIL	341,428	165,067	15,373	39,638	24,268	1,760

A   FROM THE REPORTS OF THE DIVISION OF TRANSIENT ACTIVITIES.
B   MID-MONTHLY CENSUS BEGAN FEBRUARY, 1934.
C   NO DATA AVAILABLE

TABLE 2A. AGE OF UNATTACHED TRANSIENTS REGISTERED FOR RELIEF IN 13 CITIES, MAY 1934, THROUGH APRIL 1935

Age Group	1934								1935			
	May	June	July	August	September	October	November	December	January	February	March	April
ALL PERSONS	20,233	22,590	25,152	29,090	26,898	25,160	23,412	21,835	20,613	19,008	23,953	24,268
MEDIAN AGE	28.9	27.3	25.2	26.2	27.1	28.6	28.8	29.5	28.3	28.0	27.8	28.0
Percent Distribution												
ALL PERSONS	100	100	100	100	100	100	100	100	100	100	100	100
UNDER 16 YEARS	1	1	1	1	1	*	*	*	*	*	*	*
16 TO 19 YEARS	14	18	19	19	17	15	14	12	13	14	15	15
20 TO 24 YEARS	24	25	27	27	26	25	25	25	27	27	27	27
25 TO 34 YEARS	28	26	26	26	28	28	29	29	30	30	29	27
35 TO 44 YEARS	18	16	15	15	15	17	17	18	17	16	17	17
45 TO 54 YEARS	10	9	8	8	9	10	10	10	9	9	8	9
55 TO 64 YEARS	4	4	3	3	3	4	4	4	3	3	3	4
65 YEARS AND OVER	1	1	1	1	1	1	1	2	1	1	1	1

* LESS THAN .5 PERCENT.

TABLE 2B. AGE OF HEADS OF TRANSIENT FAMILY GROUPS REGISTERED FOR RELIEF IN 13 CITIES, MAY 1934, THROUGH APRIL 1935

Age Groups	1934								1935			
	May	June	July	August	September	October	November	December	January	February	March	April
ALL PERSONS	1,641	1,827	2,048	2,277	2,122	1,908	2,064	2,137	2,261	1,669	1,759	1,769
MEDIAN AGE	34.2	34.2	34.2	33.6	33.9	33.5	33.5	34.7	33.9	33.5	33.3	34.2
Percent Distribution												
ALL PERSONS	100	100	100	100	100	100	100	100	100	100	100	100
UNDER 16 YEARS	*	*	*	*	*	*	*	–	*	–	–	*
16 TO 19 YEARS	1	1	2	2	2	2	1	1	1	1	1	1
20 TO 24 YEARS	15	14	13	16	15	15	14	14	15	16	15	14
25 TO 34 YEARS	37	38	39	37	37	39	41	38	38	39	40	39
35 TO 44 YEARS	25	25	27	26	27	24	25	25	27	25	25	25
45 TO 54 YEARS	15	14	14	13	13	14	12	14	12	12	11	14
55 TO 64 YEARS	5	5	4	4	5	5	5	6	5	5	5	5
65 YEARS AND OVER	2	2	2	2	1	1	2	2	2	2	2	2

* LESS THAN .5 PERCENT.

TABLE 2C. AGE OF RESIDENT HOMELESS PERSONS REGISTERED FOR RELIEF IN 6 CITIES[A], OCTOBER 1934, THROUGH APRIL 1935

Age Groups	1934			1935			
	October	November	December	January	February	March	April
ALL PERSONS	1317	1155	1504	1121	551	454	482
MEDIAN AGE	43.2	43.6	44.6	42.2	42.7	43.8	41.8
Percent Distribution							
ALL PERSONS	100	100	100	100	100	100	100
UNDER 16 YEARS	*	–	–	–	–	–	*
16 TO 19 YEARS	1	1	1	1	2	1	2
20 TO 24 YEARS	5	6	5	7	5	6	6
25 TO 34 YEARS	21	19	19	21	20	20	21
35 TO 44 YEARS	28	28	27	29	30	26	31
45 TO 54 YEARS	29	30	31	28	30	33	27
55 TO 64 YEARS	13	12	16	12	11	12	10
65 YEARS AND OVER	3	4	2	2	2	2	3

* LESS THAN .5 PERCENT.
A THE CITIES WERE: DENVER, JACKSONVILLE (FLA.), LOS ANGELES, MINNEAPOLIS, PITTSBURGH, AND SEATTLE.

TABLE 3. SEX RATIO OF TRANSIENTS REGISTERED FOR RELIEF IN 13 CITIES, MAY 1934, THROUGH APRIL 1935

Family Type and Sex	1934								1935			
	May	June	July	August	September	October	November	December	January	February	March	April
Unattached persons	20,235	22,790	25,152	29,090	26,898	25,160	23,412	21,835	20,613	19,008	23,953	24,268
Family group persons												
Head only	1,641	1,927	2,048	2,277	2,122	1,908	2,064	2,137	2,261	1,669	1,759	1,769
Head and others	(a)	(a)	(a)	(a)	6,562	5,958	6,535	6,591	6,917	5,071	5,318	5,538
					Percent Distribution							
Unattached persons	100.0	100.0	100.0	100.0	100.0	100.0	100.0	100.0	100.0	100.0	100.0	100.0
Male	97.4	97.6	97.7	98.0	97.8	98.0	98.0	98.2	97.7	97.9	98.1	98.0
Female	2.6	2.4	2.3	2.0	2.2	2.0	2.0	1.8	2.3	2.1	1.9	2.0
Family group persons	100.0	100.0	100.0	100.0	100.0	100.0	100.0	100.0	100.0	100.0	100.0	100.0
Head only												
Male	83.8	85.2	83.8	84.1	83.5	86.4	85.7	88.2	86.0	84.7	84.1	85.4
Female	16.2	14.8	16.2	15.9	16.5	13.6	14.3	11.8	14.0	15.3	15.9	14.6
Head and others	(a)	(a)	(a)	(a)	100.0	100.0	100.0	100.0	100.0	100.0	100.0	100.0
Male	–	–	–	–	48.5	49.3	48.8	48.7	48.3	47.7	47.9	48.6
Female	–	–	–	–	51.5	50.7	51.2	51.3	51.7	52.3	52.1	51.4

(a) DATA NOT AVAILABLE.

TABLE 4. COLOR AND NATIVITY OF TRANSIENT AND RESIDENT HOMELESS PERSONS REGISTERED FOR RELIEF IN 13 CITIES, AUGUST 1934, THROUGH APRIL 1935

Color and Nativity	1934					1935			
	August	September	October	November	December	January	February	March	April
Unattached persons	29,090	26,898	25,160	23,412	21,835	20,613	19,008	23,953	24,268
Heads of family groups	2,277	2,122	1,908	2,064	2,137	2,261	1,669	1,759	1,769
Local homeless persons[a]	1,733	1,539	1,317	1,166	1,504	1,121	551	454	482
					Percent Distribution				
Unattached persons	100	100	100	100	100	100	100	100	100
Native white	82	85	86	85	86	86	88	86	86
Foreign born white	5	5	5	5	5	4	4	4	4
Negro	12	9	8	8	7	9	7	9	8
Other	1	1	1	1	2	1	1	2	2
Heads of family groups	100	100	100	100	100	100	100	100	100
Native white	84	87	91	90	88	89	88	90	91
Foreign born white	9	6	4	4	3	4	5	4	3
Negro	5	5	4	5	6	5	6	5	5
Other	2	2	1	1	3	2	1	1	1
Local homeless persons[a]	100	100	100	100	100	100	100	100	100
Native white	65	64	55	60	53	55	62	64	65
Foreign born white	25	26	25	31	36	30	23	28	22
Negro	7	7	7	5	5	7	7	5	4
Other	3	3	3	4	6	7	8	3	9

A BASED ON RETURNS FROM 6 OF THE 13 CITIES. SEE FOOTNOTE TO TABLE 20.

TABLE 5. MARITAL STATUS OF UNATTACHED TRANSIENTS AND HEADS OF TRANSIENT FAMILY GROUPS
REGISTERED FOR RELIEF IN 13 CITIES, SEPTEMBER AND DECEMBER 1934,
AND JANUARY THROUGH APRIL 1935

MARITAL STATUS	1934		1935			
	SEPTEMBER	DECEMBER	JANUARY	FEBRUARY	MARCH	APRIL
UNATTACHED PERSONS	26,898	21,835	20,613	19,008	23,953	24,268
HEADS OF FAMILY GROUPS	2,122	2,137	2,261	1,669	1,759	1,769
			Percent Distribution			
UNATTACHED PERSONS	100	100	100	100	100	100
SINGLE	80	80	79	80	81	80
MARRIED	6	6	6	5	6	6
WIDOWED OR DIVORCED	10	10	10	10	9	9
SEPARATED	4	4	5	5	4	5
HEADS OF FAMILY GROUPS	100	100	100	100	100	100
SINGLE	3	1	1	1	2	1
MARRIED	83	88	86	86	84	85
WIDOWED OR DIVORCED	7	6	7	7	8	8
SEPARATED	7	5	6	6	6	6

TABLE 6. SEX AND MARITAL STATUS OF TRANSIENTS REGISTERED FOR RELIEF IN 13 CITIES, SEPTEMBER, 1934

SEX AND MARITAL STATUS	UNATTACHED TRANSIENTS	FAMILY GROUPS	
		HEADS	OTHERS
ALL PERSONS	26,898	2,122	4,440
MALE	26,306	1,772	1,411
FEMALE	592	350	3,029
		Percent Distribution	
ALL PERSONS	100	100	100
MALE	98	84	32
FEMALE	2	16	68
MALE	100	100	100
SINGLE	81	2	98
MARRIED	6	95	2
WIDOWED OR DIVORCED	9	2	*
SEPARATED	4	1	*
FEMALE	100	100	100
SINGLE	39	8	43
MARRIED	14	22	55
WIDOWED OR DIVORCED	31	34	1
SEPARATED	16	36	1

* LESS THAN .5 PERCENT.

TABLE 7A. AGE, SEX, AND MARITAL STATUS OF UNATTACHED TRANSIENTS REGISTERED FOR RELIEF IN 13 CITIES, SEPTEMBER 1934

Age and Sex	ALL CLASSES	SINGLE	MARRIED	WIDOWED OR DIVORCED	SEPARATED
MALE	26,306	21,308	1,578	2,368	1,052
FEMALE	592	231	83	183	95
			Percent Distribution		
MALE	100	100	100	100	100
Under 16 years	1	1	*	-	-
16 to 19 years	17	21	1	*	1
20 to 24 years	26	30	11	3	9
25 to 34 years	27	27	37	22	38
35 to 44 years	15	12	28	31	30
45 years and over	14	9	23	44	22
Not ascertainable	*	-	-	-	-
FEMALE	100	100	100	100	100
Under 16 years	4	9	1	-	1
16 to 19 years	11	23	3	2	9
20 to 24 years	24	34	34	5	21
25 to 34 years	22	19	22	20	32
35 to 44 years	16	7	21	23	21
45 years and over	23	8	18	49	16
Not ascertainable	*	-	1	1	-

* LESS THAN .5 PERCENT.

TABLE 7B. AGE, SEX, AND MARITAL STATUS OF HEADS OF TRANSIENT FAMILY GROUPS REGISTERED FOR RELIEF IN 13 CITIES, SEPTEMBER 1934

Age and Sex	ALL CLASSES	SINGLE	MARRIED	WIDOWED OR DIVORCED	SEPARATED
MALE	1,772	33	1,681	36	22
FEMALE	350	29	77	119	125
			Percent Distribution		
MALE	100	(A)	100	(A)	(A)
Under 16 years	-	-	-	-	-
16 to 19 years	2	-	2	-	-
20 to 24 years	16	-	16	-	-
25 to 34 years	39	-	39	-	-
35 to 44 years	26	-	26	-	-
45 years and over	18	-	17	-	-
Not ascertainable	*	-	-	-	-
FEMALE	100	(A)	100	100	100
Under 16 years	*	-	-	-	1
16 to 19 years	4	-	-	-	4
20 to 24 years	18	-	23	5	23
25 to 34 years	30	-	26	18	43
35 to 44 years	28	-	39	36	19
45 years and over	20	-	12	41	10
Not ascertainable	-	-	-	-	-

* LESS THAN .5 PERCENT.
(A) PERCENTAGES NOT COMPUTED BECAUSE OF SMALL NUMBERS INVOLVED.

TABLE 7C. AGE, SEX, AND MARITAL STATUS OF OTHER PERSONS THAN HEADS OF TRANSIENT FAMILY GROUPS REGISTERED FOR RELIEF IN 13 CITIES, SEPTEMBER 1934

AGE AND SEX	ALL CLASSES	SINGLE	MARRIED	WIDOWED OR DIVORCED	SEPARATED
MALE	1,411	1,377	25	6	3
FEMALE	3,029	1,303	1,673	38	15
		Percent Distribution			
MALE	100	100	(A)	(A)	(A)
UNDER 16 YEARS	83	85	-	-	-
16 TO 19 YEARS	9	9	-	-	-
20 TO 24 YEARS	4	4	-	-	-
25 TO 34 YEARS	2	2	-	-	-
35 TO 44 YEARS	1	*	-	-	-
45 YEARS AND OVER	1	*	-	-	-
NOT ASCERTAINABLE	-	-	-	-	-
FEMALE	100	100	100	(A)	(A)
UNDER 16 YEARS	39	88	2	-	-
16 TO 19 YEARS	10	8	11	-	-
20 TO 24 YEARS	15	3	25	-	-
25 TO 34 YEARS	20	1	36	-	-
35 TO 44 YEARS	10	*	18	-	-
45 YEARS AND OVER	6	*	8	-	-
NOT ASCERTAINABLE	*	-	*	-	-

* LESS THAN .5 PERCENT.
(A) PERCENTAGES NOT COMPUTED BECAUSE OF SMALL NUMBERS INVOLVED.

TABLE 8A. COLOR AND NATIVITY AND MARITAL STATUS OF UNATTACHED TRANSIENTS REGISTERED FOR RELIEF IN 13 CITIES, SEPTEMBER 1934

COLOR AND NATIVITY	NUMBER	PERCENT	PERCENT DISTRIBUTION BY MARITAL STATUS				
			TOTAL	SINGLE	MARRIED	WIDOWED OR DIVORCED	SEPARATED
ALL PERSONS	26,898	100	100	80	6	10	4
NATIVE WHITE	22,954	85	100	81	5	10	4
FOREIGN BORN WHITE	1,321	5	100	76	7	13	4
NEGRO	2,340	9	100	78	7	7	8
OTHER	283	1	100	86	6	5	3

TABLE 8B. COLOR AND NATIVITY AND MARITAL STATUS OF HEADS OF TRANSIENT FAMILY GROUPS REGISTERED FOR RELIEF IN 13 CITIES, SEPTEMBER 1934

COLOR AND NATIVITY	NUMBER	PERCENT	PERCENT DISTRIBUTION BY MARITAL STATUS				
			TOTAL	SINGLE	MARRIED	WIDOWED OR DIVORCED	SEPARATED
ALL PERSONS	2,122	100	100	3	83	7	7
NATIVE WHITE	1,847	87	100	2	84	7	7
FOREIGN BORN WHITE	127	6	100	1	82	10	7
NEGRO	106	5	100	8	66	11	15
OTHER	42	2	(A)	-	-	-	-

(A) PERCENTAGES NOT COMPUTED BECAUSE OF SMALL NUMBERS INVOLVED.

TABLE 9.   SIZE OF TRANSIENT FAMILY GROUPS REGISTERED FOR RELIEF IN 13 CITIES, SEPTEMBER 1934,
THROUGH APRIL 1935

SIZE OF FAMILY GROUP	1934				1935			
	SEPTEMBER	OCTOBER	NOVEMBER	DECEMBER	JANUARY	FEBRUARY	MARCH	APRIL
ALL FAMILY GROUPS	2,122	1,908	2,064	2,137	2,261	1,669	1,759	1,769
ALL FAMILY GROUP PERSONS	6,562	5,963	6,520	6,559	5,917	5,071	5,318	5,538
AVERAGE SIZE OF FAMILY	3.1	3.1	3.2	3.1	3.1	3.0	3.0	3.1
				Percent Distribution				
ALL FAMILY GROUPS	100	100	100	100	100	100	100	100
2 PERSON FAMILIES	48	47	45	49	48	51	51	51
3 PERSON FAMILIES	22	24	25	23	24	23	22	20
4 PERSON FAMILIES	14	14	14	15	14	13	13	14
5 PERSON FAMILIES	8	7	8	7	7	6	7	7
6 PERSON FAMILIES	3	4	4	3	3	3	3	4
7 PERSON FAMILIES	2	2	2	1	2	2	2	2
8 PERSON FAMILIES	2	1	1	1	1	1	1	1
9 OR MORE PERSON FAMILIES	1	1	1	1	1	1	1	1

TABLE 10.   EDUCATION OF TRANSIENT AND RESIDENT HOMELESS PERSONS REGISTERED FOR RELIEF IN 13 CITIES,
SEPTEMBER 1934

EDUCATION	TRANSIENT		RESIDENT HOMELESS[A]
	UNATTACHED PERSONS	HEADS OF FAMILY GROUPS	UNATTACHED PERSONS
ALL PERSONS	26,898	2,122	1,539
		Percent Distribution	
ALL PERSONS	100.0	100.C	100.0
NONE	2.0	3.3	6.1
GRADE SCHOOL	56.1	59.6	71.1
INCOMPLETED	29.8	34.7	43.2
COMPLETED	26.3	24.9	27.9
HIGH SCHOOL	38.0	32.1	20.2
INCOMPLETED	25.1	19.1	13.2
COMPLETED	12.9	13.0	7.0
COLLEGE	3.7	4.6	2.3
INCOMPLETED	2.8	3.2	1.6
COMPLETED	0.9	1.4	0.7
POST GRADUATE	0.2	0.2	0.2
NOT ASCERTAINABLE		0.2	0.1
MEDIAN GRADE COMPLETED	8	8	8

A   BASED ON RETURNS FROM 6 OF THE 13 CITIES.   SEE FOOTNOTE TO TABLE 2C.
*   LESS THAN .05 PERCENT.

TABLE 11. EDUCATION OF UNATTACHED TRANSIENTS REGISTERED FOR RELIEF IN 13 CITIES, SEPTEMBER 1934, BY COLOR AND NATIVITY

EDUCATION	ALL RACES	NATIVE WHITE	FOREIGN BORN WHITE	NEGRO	MEXICAN	OTHER
ALL PERSONS						
			Percent Distribution			
ALL PERSONS	100.0	100.0	100.0	100.0	100.0	(A)
NONE	2.0	1.0	5.8	9.1	8.6	–
GRADE SCHOOL	*56.1*	*53.7*	*71.8*	*68.5*	*72.8*	–
INCOMPLETED	29.8	26.1	46.7	53.1	57.1	–
COMPLETED	26.3	27.6	25.1	15.4	15.7	–
HIGH SCHOOL	*38.0*	*41.1*	*19.5*	*21.6*	*18.1*	–
INCOMPLETED	25.1	27.0	10.8	17.1	16.1	–
COMPLETED	12.9	14.1	8.7	4.5	2.0	–
COLLEGE	*3.7*	*4.0*	*2.5*	*0.8*	*0.5*	–
INCOMPLETED	2.8	3.1	1.4	0.7	–	–
COMPLETED	0.9	0.9	1.1	0.1	0.5	–
POST GRADUATE	0.2	0.2	0.4	*	–	–
NOT ASCERTAINABLE	*	*	–	–	–	–

(A) PERCENTAGE NOT COMPUTED BECAUSE OF SMALL NUMBERS INVOLVED.
* LESS THAN .05 PERCENT.

TABLE 12A. AGE AND EDUCATION OF UNATTACHED TRANSIENTS REGISTERED FOR RELIEF IN 13 CITIES, SEPTEMBER 1934

EDUCATION	ALL AGES	UNDER 16 YEARS	16–17 YEARS	18–19 YEARS	20–24 YEARS	25–34 YEARS	35–44 YEARS	45 YEARS & OVER	N.A.
ALL PERSONS	26,898	172	1,171	3,345	6,909	7,457	4,138	3,705	1
					Percent Distribution				
ALL PERSONS	100.0	100.0	100.0	100.0	100.0	100.0	100.0	100.0	(A)
NONE	2.0	1.2	1.0	0.6	1.1	1.6	2.9	4.9	–
GRADE SCHOOL	*56.1*	*73.7*	*53.5*	*45.6*	*46.4*	*56.6*	*65.1*	*72.3*	–
INCOMPLETED	29.8	55.1	28.0	23.3	22.4	29.0	35.6	43.6	–
COMPLETED	26.3	18.6	25.5	22.3	24.0	27.6	29.5	28.7	–
HIGH SCHOOL	*38.0*	*25.1*	*45.4*	*53.1*	*48.7*	*36.5*	*26.9*	*18.7*	–
INCOMPLETED	25.1	24.5	41.4	40.5	31.9	22.5	15.9	9.5	–
COMPLETED	12.9	0.6	4.0	12.6	16.8	14.0	11.0	9.2	–
COLLEGE	*3.7*	–	*0.1*	*0.7*	*3.8*	*5.0*	*4.8*	*3.5*	–
INCOMPLETED	2.8	–	0.1	0.7	3.3	3.9	3.2	2.0	–
COMPLETED	0.9	–	–	*	0.5	1.1	1.6	1.5	–
POST GRADUATE	0.2	–	–	*	*	0.3	0.3	0.4	–
NOT ASCERTAINABLE	*	–	–	*	*	*	*	0.2	–

(A) PERCENTAGE NOT COMPUTED BECAUSE OF SMALL NUMBERS INVOLVED.
* LESS THAN .05 PERCENT.

TABLE 12B. AGE AND EDUCATION OF HEADS OF TRANSIENT FAMILY GROUPS REGISTERED
FOR RELIEF IN 13 CITIES, SEPTEMBER 1934

EDUCATION	ALL AGES	UNDER 16 YEARS	16–17 YEARS	18–19 YEARS	20–24 YEARS	25–34 YEARS	35–44 YEARS	45 YEARS & OVER
ALL PERSONS	2,122	2	5	33	330	784	581	387
				Percent Distribution				
ALL PERSONS	100.0	(A)	(A)	(A)	100.0	100.0	100.0	100.0
NONE	3.3	–	–	–	0.9	2.9	3.1	6.7
GRADE SCHOOL	59.6	–	–	–	51.8	57.1	63.4	65.0
INCOMPLETED	34.7	–	–	–	30.0	33.4	36.5	37.5
COMPLETED	24.9	–	–	–	21.8	23.7	26.9	27.5
HIGH SCHOOL	32.1	–	–	–	45.2	35.0	27.9	21.4
INCOMPLETED	19.1	–	–	–	28.2	21.1	16.1	11.6
COMPLETED	13.0	–	–	–	17.0	13.9	11.8	9.8
COLLEGE	4.6	–	–	–	2.1	5.0	5.2	5.4
INCOMPLETED	3.2	–	–	–	2.1	4.0	3.3	2.8
COMPLETED	1.4	–	–	–	–	1.0	1.9	2.6
POST GRADUATE	0.2	–	–	–	–	–	0.2	1.0
NOT ASCERTAINABLE	0.2	–	–	–	–	–	0.2	0.5

(A) PERCENTAGE NOT COMPUTED BECAUSE OF SMALL NUMBERS INVOLVED.

TABLE 13. EMPLOYMENT STATUS OF TRANSIENTS REGISTERED FOR RELIEF IN 13 CITIES, OCTOBER 1934
THROUGH APRIL 1935

EMPLOYMENT STATUS	1934			1935			
	OCTOBER	NOVEMBER	DECEMBER	JANUARY	FEBRUARY	MARCH	APRIL
UNATTACHED PERSONS	25,160	23,412	21,835	20,613	19,008	23,953	24,268
HEADS OF FAMILY GROUPS	1,908	2,064	2,137	2,261	1,669	1,759	1,769
			Percent Distribution				
UNATTACHED PERSONS	100	100	100	100	100	100	100
EMPLOYED	1	1	1	1	*	1	*
UNEMPLOYED	99	99	99	99	100	99	100
ABLE AND WILLING TO WORK	95	95	95	95	96	96	96
UNABLE TO WORK	4	4	4	4	4	3	4
TEMPORARY DISABILITY	2	2	2	2	2	1	2
PERMANENT DISABILITY	1	1	1	1	1	1	1
HOUSEWORK (UNPAID)	*	*	*	*	*	*	*
TOO OLD	1	1	1	1	1	1	1
OTHER REASONS	*	*	*	*	*	*	*
HEADS OF FAMILY GROUPS	100	100	100	100	100	100	100
EMPLOYED	2	2	2	3	2	3	3
UNEMPLOYED	98	98	97	96	98	97	97
ABLE AND WILLING TO WORK	91	88	89	87	88	86	86
UNABLE TO WORK	7	10	8	9	10	11	11
TEMPORARY DISABILITY	2	3	2	2	2	1	2
PERMANENT DISABILITY	2	2	2	1	2	2	2
HOUSEWORK (UNPAID)	3	3	3	5	5	6	5
TOO OLD	*	1	1	1	1	1	2
OTHER REASONS	*	1	*	–	*	*	*
EMPLOYMENT STATUS NOT ASCERTAINABLE	–	–	1	1	*	–	–

* LESS THAN .5 PERCENT.

TABLE 14. WORK HISTORY OF TRANSIENTS REGISTERED FOR RELIEF IN 13 CITIES, SEPTEMBER 1934, THROUGH APRIL 1935

Work History	1934				1935			
	September	October	November	December	January	February	March	April
Unattached persons	26,757	25,160	23,412	21,835	20,613	19,008	23,953	24,268
Heads of family groups	2,122	1,908	2,964	2,137	2,261	1,669	1,759	1,769
Percent Distribution								
Unattached persons	100.0	100.0	100.0	100.0	100.0	100.0	100.0	100.0
Never worked	5.2	5.3	5.2	4.6	4.6	4.8	4.3	3.8
No usual occupation	5.6	7.0	8.9	9.4	11.3	12.4	13.4	14.9
With usual occupation	89.1	87.2	85.6	85.7	83.6	82.5	81.6	81.1
Not ascertainable	0.1	0.5	0.3	0.3	0.5	0.3	0.7	0.2
Heads of family groups	100.0	100.0	100.0	100.0	100.0	100.0	100.0	100.0
Never worked	3.7	4.5	4.9	3.7	6.5	6.6	6.9	5.7
No usual occupation	1.1	3.8	2.2	2.6	3.6	4.4	5.4	4.7
With usual occupation	95.0	91.1	92.4	93.4	89.0	88.6	87.3	89.3
Not ascertainable	0.2	0.6	0.5	0.3	0.9	0.4	0.4	0.3

TABLE 15. WORK HISTORY OF TRANSIENTS REGISTERED FOR RELIEF IN 13 CITIES, CLASSIFIED BY SEX, JANUARY THROUGH APRIL 1935

Work History	Male				Female			
	January	February	March	April	January	February	March	April
Unattached persons	20,140	18,601	23,499	23,777	473	407	454	491
Heads of family groups	1,944	1,415	1,480	1,511	317	254	279	258
Percent Distribution								
Unattached persons	100.0	100.0	100.0	100.0	100.0	100.0	100.0	100.0
Never worked	4.2	4.3	3.9	3.3	25.3	26.8	25.8	25.0
No usual occupation	11.3	12.4	13.5	15.0	8.6	10.6	10.1	12.5
With usual occupation	84.0	83.0	81.9	81.5	65.3	61.1	63.4	61.3
Not ascertainable	0.5	0.3	0.7	0.2	0.8	1.5	0.7	1.2
Heads of family groups	100.0	100.0	100.0	100.0	100.0	100.0	100.0	100.0
Never worked	1.2	0.5	1.0	0.5	39.3	40.6	38.0	36.4
No usual occupation	2.5	2.6	3.9	2.6	10.4	14.2	13.6	17.4
With usual occupation	95.4	96.5	94.7	96.6	49.4	44.8	48.0	45.8
Not ascertainable	0.9	0.4	0.4	0.3	0.9	0.4	0.4	0.4

TABLE 16. USUAL OCCUPATION OF TRANSIENTS REGISTERED FOR RELIEF IN 13 CITIES, CLASSIFIED BY FAMILY
TYPE, FOR JANUARY THROUGH APRIL, 1935

USUAL OCCUPATION	1935			
	JANUARY	FEBRUARY	MARCH	APRIL
UNATTACHED PERSONS	17,215	15,681	19,539	19,673
HEADS OF FAMILY GROUPS	2,012	1,479	1,536	1,578
	Percent Distribution			
UNATTACHED PERSONS	100.0	100.0	100.0	100.0
PROFESSIONAL PERSONS	2.4	2.5	2.3	2.0
SEMI-PROFESSIONAL AND RECREATIONAL WORKERS	0.4	0.2	0.3	0.3
PROPRIETORS, MANAGERS AND OFFICIALS	3.5	3.5	3.5	3.4
CLERICAL WORKERS	5.0	5.3	5.0	4.9
SALES PERSONS	6.3	6.1	6.2	5.7
TELEPHONE, TELEGRAPH AND RADIO OPERATORS	0.2	0.3	0.3	0.3
SKILLED WORKERS	17.1	16.9	16.6	16.3
SEMI-SKILLED WORKERS	23.2	23.0	24.3	23.8
UNSKILLED WORKERS	30.7	30.9	30.6	32.7
SERVANTS AND ALLIED WORKERS	11.2	11.3	10.9	10.6
HEADS OF FAMILY GROUPS	100.0	100.0	100.0	100.0
PROFESSIONAL PERSONS	3.8	3.9	5.0	4.0
SEMI-PROFESSIONAL AND RECREATIONAL WORKERS	0.8	0.3	0.6	0.4
PROPRIETORS, MANAGERS AND OFFICIALS	14.6	14.6	12.8	14.1
CLERICAL WORKERS	3.8	2.7	3.8	3.9
SALES PERSONS	8.2	7.6	7.4	8.2
TELEPHONE, TELEGRAPH AND RADIO OPERATORS	0.2	0.8	0.2	*
SKILLED WORKERS	19.2	20.0	19.1	18.8
SEMI-SKILLED WORKERS	19.8	20.0	22.1	20.6
UNSKILLED WORKERS	21.4	22.0	20.6	21.3
SERVANTS AND ALLIED WORKERS	8.2	8.1	8.4	8.7

* LESS THAN .05 PERCENT.

TABLE 17. COMPARISON OF TRANSIENT AND RESIDENT RELIEF UNEMPLOYED WITH TOTAL GAINFULLY EMPLOYED
POPULATION IN 1930, PERCENT DISTRIBUTION

USUAL OCCUPATION	TRANSIENT REGISTRA-TIONS[A], 13 CITIES APRIL, 1935	RESIDENT RELIEF REGISTRATIONS, 79 CITIES, MAY, 1934	ALL GAINFUL WORKERS[B] 1930 U.S. CENSUS
ALL PERSONS	100.0	100.0	100.0
PROFESSIONAL PERSONS	2.2	2.1	6.1
SEMI-PROFESSIONAL AND RECREATIONAL WORKERS	0.3	0.2	0.4
PROPRIETORS, MANAGERS AND OFFICIALS	4.2	3.3	18.9
CLERICAL WORKERS	4.8	5.4	8.6
SALES PERSONS	5.9	5.4	7.3
TELEPHONE, TELEGRAPH AND RADIO OPERATORS	0.3	0.4	0.7
SKILLED WORKERS	16.5	18.1	13.4
SEMI-SKILLED WORKERS	23.6	27.8	16.6
UNSKILLED WORKERS	31.8	21.0	21.1
SERVANTS AND ALLIED WORKERS	10.4	16.3	6.9

A   UNATTACHED PERSONS AND HEADS OF FAMILY GROUPS.
B   SEE FIFTEENTH CENSUS POPULATION, VOL. V, TABLE 3.

TABLE 18.   USUAL OCCUPATION OF TRANSIENTS REGISTERED FOR RELIEF IN 13 CITIES, CLASSIFIED BY SEX, JANUARY THROUGH APRIL 1935

USUAL OCCUPATION	MALE				FEMALE			
	JANUARY	FEBRUARY	MARCH	APRIL	JANUARY	FEBRUARY	MARCH	APRIL
UNATTACHED PERSONS	16,906	15,434	19,251	19,372	309	247	288	301
HEADS OF FAMILY GROUPS	1,855	1,365	1,402	1,460	197	114	134	118
				Percent Distribution				
UNATTACHED PERSONS	100.0	100.0	100.0	100.0	100.0	100.0	100.0	100.0
PROFESSIONAL PERSONS	2.3	2.3	2.2	1.9	5.8	10.1	8.7	6.3
SEMI-PROFESSIONAL AND RECREATIONAL WORKERS	0.4	0.2	0.3	0.3	1.3	0.4	-	0.6
PROPRIETORS, MANAGERS AND OFFICIALS	3.5	3.5	3.5	3.4	1.9	2.4	2.8	2.7
CLERICAL WORKERS	4.9	5.3	4.9	4.8	8.1	6.9	10.1	10.3
SALES PERSONS	6.2	6.0	6.1	5.7	9.1	10.1	7.6	7.0
TELEPHONE, TELEGRAPH AND RADIO OPERATORS	0.2	0.3	0.2	0.2	1.3	2.4	2.4	2.0
SKILLED WORKERS	17.5	17.2	16.9	16.6	1.0	0.4	0.7	0.3
SEMI-SKILLED WORKERS	25.2	23.0	24.3	23.8	24.3	25.1	26.0	25.9
UNSKILLED WORKERS	31.2	31.4	31.1	33.2	2.6	2.9	1.7	2.3
SERVANTS AND ALLIED WORKERS	10.6	10.8	10.5	10.1	44.6	39.3	40.0	42.6
HEADS OF FAMILY GROUPS	100.0	100.0	100.0	100.0	100.0	100.0	100.0	100.0
PROFESSIONAL PERSONS	3.6	3.8	4.5	3.9	7.0	4.4	10.4	5.1
SEMI-PROFESSIONAL AND RECREATIONAL WORKERS	0.9	0.3	0.6	0.5	-	-	-	-
PROPRIETORS, MANAGERS AND OFFICIALS	15.2	15.4	13.5	15.0	6.4	5.3	5.2	3.4
CLERICAL WORKERS	3.6	2.6	3.7	3.5	7.0	3.5	4.5	9.3
SALES PERSONS	8.3	7.4	7.3	8.1	7.0	9.6	8.2	9.3
TELEPHONE, TELEGRAPH AND RADIO OPERATORS	0.1	0.6	0.1	0.1	2.6	3.5	1.5	-
SKILLED WORKERS	20.8	21.5	20.8	20.1	-	1.8	1.5	1.7
SEMI-SKILLED WORKERS	19.1	18.7	21.5	20.1	28.0	36.0	28.4	27.1
UNSKILLED WORKERS	22.5	23.6	22.4	22.2	7.6	3.5	3.0	7.6
SERVANTS AND ALLIED WORKERS	5.9	6.1	5.6	6.5	34.4	32.4	37.3	36.5

TABLE 19.   USUAL OCCUPATIONS OF TRANSIENTS REGISTERED FOR RELIEF IN 13 CITIES, FEBRUARY 1935

Occupation	Unattached Persons	Heads of Family Groups
With usual occupation	15,681	1,479
	Percent Distribution	
With usual occupation	100.0	100.0
Professional persons:	2.5	3.9
Actors and showmen	0.6	0.6
Artists, sculptors, and teachers of art	0.1	–
Designers, draftsmen, inventors, and architects	0.1	0.2
Musicians and teachers of music	0.5	1.0
Physicians, dentists, veterinary surgeons, and osteopaths	0.1	0.1
Teachers (school and college)	0.2	0.3
Technical engineers and chemists	0.3	0.6
Trained nurses	0.2	–
Other professional persons: Clergymen; authors, editors and reporters, lawyers, judges and justices; photographers; county agents, farm demonstrators; librarians; social and welfare workers; and all other professional workers	0.4	1.1
Semi-professional and recreational workers:	0.2	0.3
Abstractors, apprentices to professional persons, chiropractors, healers, officials of lodges, etc., religious workers, and technicians	*	0.2
Proprietors, managers and officials in recreational pursuits	0.1	0.1
Other semi-professional and recreational workers	0.1	–
Proprietors, managers, and officials:	3.5	14.6
Agricultural proprietors and managers	1.3	9.3
Builders and building contractors	*	0.4
Hotel and restaurant keepers and managers	0.3	0.7
Manufacturers, proprietors, managers and officials (not elsewhere classified)	0.7	1.7
Wholesale and retail dealers	1.2	2.5
Clerical workers:	5.3	2.7
Bookkeepers, cashiers, and accountants	1.2	0.8
Clerical workers (proper)	3.5	1.6
Quasi-clerical workers (express agents, express messengers, railway clerks, mail carriers, ticket and station agents, baggagemen and freight agents)	*	0.1
Office boys, telegraph and other messengers	0.3	–
Stenographers and typists	0.3	0.2
Sales persons:	6.1	7.6
Advertising agents	0.2	0.3
Agents, collectors and creditmen	0.1	0.4
Commercial travelers	0.3	0.3
Newsboys	0.2	–
Real estate and insurance agents	0.3	0.3
Salesmen and saleswomen (proper)	5.0	6.3
Telephone, telegraph and radio operators:	0.3	0.8
Telephone operators	0.1	0.3
Telegraph and radio operators	0.2	0.5
Skilled workers:	16.9	20.0
Blacksmiths, forgemen, and hammermen	0.4	0.6
Boilermakers	0.2	0.2
Brick and stone masons and tile layers	0.4	0.3
Cabinet makers	0.1	–
Carpenters	1.4	1.6
Electricians	0.8	0.6
Engineers (stationary), cranemen, hoistmen, etc.	0.7	0.4
Locomotive engineers and firemen	0.3	0.7
Machinists, millwrights, and tool makers	1.4	1.5
Mechanics (not otherwise specified)	2.6	4.8
Molders, founders, and casters (metal)	0.3	0.2
Painters, enamelers, varnishers (bldg.), and paper hangers	3.0	4.7
Painters, glaziers, enamelers, and varnishers in factories	0.4	0.3
Pattern and model makers	*	–
Plasterers and cement finishers	0.3	0.5
Plumbers and gas and steam fitters	0.9	0.6
Rollers and roll hands (metal)	0.1	–
Roofers and slaters	0.2	0.1
Sawyers	0.2	0.4

TABLE 19. (CONTINUED)

OCCUPATION	UNATTACHED PERSONS	HEADS OF FAMILY GROUPS
SKILLED WORKERS: (CONT'D)		
SHOEMAKERS AND COBBLERS (NOT IN FACTORY)	0.3	0.1
STRUCTURAL IRON WORKERS (BLDG.)	0.5	0.3
TAILORS AND TAILORESSES	0.3	0.1
TINSMITHS AND COPPERSMITHS	0.3	0.2
UPHOLSTERERS	0.2	0.1
SKILLED WORKERS IN PRINTING, PUBLISHING, AND ENGRAVING	0.6	0.1
SKILLED WORKERS (NOT ELSEWHERE CLASSIFIED)	0.5	0.8
FOREMEN, OVERSEERS AND INSPECTORS (EXCEPT INSPECTORS AND FOREMEN IN LUMBER CAMPS, AND INSPECTORS IN FACTORIES, AND FOREMEN IN LAUNDRIES AND CLEANING ESTABLISHMENTS)	0.5	0.8
SEMI-SKILLED WORKERS	23.0	20.0
BAKERS	0.7	0.9
BARBERS, HAIRDRESSERS, AND MANICURISTS	0.8	0.7
BOARDING AND LODGING HOUSEKEEPERS	•	0.1
BOILERS, WASHERS AND ENGINE HOSTLERS	•	-
BRAKEMEN	0.3	0.1
CHAUFFEURS, DELIVERYMEN, TRUCK AND TRACTOR DRIVERS	7.4	6.5
ASSISTANTS AND ATTENDANTS TO PROFESSIONAL PERSONS	•	-
ATTENDANTS AND HELPERS (PROFESSIONAL SERVICE, RECREATION, AND AMUSEMENT)	0.4	0.1
LABORERS (PROFESSIONAL SERVICE, RECREATION, AND AMUSEMENT)	0.2	0.1
DRESSMAKERS, SEAMSTRESSES AND MILLINERS	•	0.1
FILERS, GRINDERS, BUFFERS, AND POLISHERS (METAL)	0.3	0.3
HOUSEKEEPERS, STEWARDS, AND PRACTICAL NURSES	0.6	1.2
OILERS OF MACHINERY	0.2	0.2
OPERATIVES:	8.1	7.5
OPERATIVES IN BUILDING TRADES	0.1	0.1
OPERATIVES IN CIGAR FACTORIES	0.1	0.1
OPERATIVES IN CLOTHING FACTORIES	0.3	0.5
OPERATIVES IN OTHER FACTORIES, LAUNDRIES, AND DRY-CLEANING ESTABLISHMENTS	7.6	6.8
SAILORS, DECK HANDS, BOATMEN, AND CANALMEN	1.7	-
SWITCHMEN, FLAGMEN, AND YARDMEN	0.4	0.4
TELEGRAPH AND TELEPHONE LINEMEN	0.3	0.3
WATCHMEN, GUARDS AND DOORKEEPERS	0.2	0.1
OTHER WORKERS (SEMI-SKILLED)	1.4	1.6
UNSKILLED WORKERS:	30.9	22.0
DRAYMEN, TEAMSTERS, AND EXPRESSMEN	0.4	0.3
FARM LABORERS:	14.0	9.7
GENERAL FARM	8.4	5.5
GRAIN FARM	0.8	0.4
STOCK FARM	0.9	0.5
COTTON FARM	1.2	1.1
TOBACCO FARM	0.1	0.1
DAIRY FARM	0.8	0.5
POULTRY FARM	0.1	0.1
FRUIT AND BERRY FARM (VINEYARDS AND NUTS)	0.5	0.3
TRUCK FARM	0.5	0.5
NURSERIES	0.1	0.2
GREEN HOUSES	•	•
SMALL ANIMAL BREEDING FARMS	•	-
OTHER SINGLE CROP FARMS (SUGAR BEET, CRANBERRY, HOP, ETC.)	0.3	0.3
GARDENERS, LANDSCAPE LABORERS, ETC.	0.3	0.2
FIREMEN (EXCEPT LOCOMOTIVE AND FIRE DEPARTMENT)	0.9	0.3
FISHERMEN AND OYSTERMEN	0.2	0.1
FURNACEMEN, SMELTERMEN, HEATERS AND PUDDLERS	0.1	0.1
LONGSHOREMEN AND STEVEDORES	0.4	0.3
LUMBERMEN, RAFTSMEN, AND WOODCHOPPERS	0.8	0.6
MINERS, OIL, GAS, AND SALT WELL OPERATIVES	2.9	2.4
LABORERS (NOT ELSEWHERE CLASSIFIED)	11.2	8.2
SERVANTS AND ALLIED WORKERS:	11.3	8.1
BOOTBLACKS	0.1	-
CHARWOMEN	0.1	0.2
ELEVATOR TENDERS	0.1	0.2
JANITORS AND SEXTONS	0.5	0.4
PORTERS	0.6	0.2
SERVANTS	7.0	5.6
WAITERS, WAITRESSES AND BARTENDERS	2.9	1.5

* LESS THAN .05 PERCENT.

TABLE 20A. WORK HISTORY OF TRANSIENTS REGISTERED FOR RELIEF IN 13 CITIES, CLASSIFIED BY SEX AND AGE GROUPS, APRIL 1935

Work History	Male						Female					
	Total	Under 20 Years	20-24 Years	25-34 Years	35-44 Years	45 Years & Over	Total	Under 20 Years	20-24 Years	25-34 Years	35-44 Years	45 Years & Over
UNATTACHED PERSONS												
Number	23,777	3634	6417	6510	4005	3211	491	84	109	110	81	107
Percent	100.0	15.3	27.0	27.4	16.8	13.5	100.0	17.1	22.2	22.4	16.5	21.8
HEADS OF FAMILY GROUPS												
Number	1511	13	220	589	380	309	258	7	34	90	67	60
Percent	100.0	0.9	14.6	39.0	25.1	20.4	100.0	2.7	13.2	34.9	26.0	23.2
				Percent Distribution								
UNATTACHED PERSONS	100.0	100.0	100.0	100.0	100.0	100.0	100.0	100.0	100.0	100.0	100.0	100.0
NEVER WORKED	3.3	14.5	2.7	0.9	0.6	0.3	25.1	40.5	19.3	16.7	23.5	29.0
NO USUAL OCCUPATION	15.0	51.0	19.9	4.4	2.3	1.6	12.4	23.8	11.9	12.0	9.9	6.5
WITH USUAL OCCUPATION	81.5	34.5	77.4	94.5	96.9	97.4	61.3	35.7	67.9	69.5	66.6	61.7
NOT ASCERTAINABLE	0.2	-	*	0.2	0.2	0.7	1.2	-	0.9	1.8	-	2.8
HEADS OF FAMILY GROUPS	100.0	(a)	100.0	100.0	100.0	100.0	100.0	(a)	(a)	100.0	100.0	100.0
NEVER WORKED	0.5	-	-	0.7	0.5	-	36.4	-	-	38.9	28.3	36.7
NO USUAL OCCUPATION	2.6	-	8.6	2.4	1.1	-	17.4	-	-	13.3	19.4	16.7
WITH USUAL OCCUPATION	96.6	-	91.4	96.7	97.6	99.7	45.8	-	-	46.7	52.3	45.6
NOT ASCERTAINABLE	0.3	-	-	0.2	0.8	0.3	0.4	-	-	1.1	-	-

LESS THAN .05 PERCENT.
(A) PERCENTAGE NOT COMPUTED BECAUSE OF SMALL NUMBERS INVOLVED.

TABLE 20B. USUAL OCCUPATIONS OF TRANSIENTS REGISTERED FOR RELIEF IN 13 CITIES, CLASSIFIED BY SEX, AND BY AGE GROUPS, APRIL 1935

Usual Occupations	Male						Female					
	All Ages	Under 20 Years	20-24 Years	25-34 Years	35-44 Years	45 Years & Over	All Ages	Under 20 Years	20-24 Years	25-34 Years	35-44 Years	45 Years & Over
UNATTACHED PERSONS	19,372	1253	4965	6150	3875	3129	301	30	74	77	54	66
HEADS OF FAMILY GROUPS	1,460	10	201	570	371	308	118	2	11	42	35	28
				Percent Distribution								
UNATTACHED PERSONS	100.0	100.0	100.0	100.0	100.0	100.0	100.0	(a)	100.0	100.0	100.0	100.0
PROFESSIONAL PERSONS	1.9	1.3	1.7	2.3	2.2	1.4	6.3	-	5.8	3.9	11.1	4.5
SEMI-PROFESSIONAL AND RECREATIONAL WORKERS	0.3	0.2	0.2	0.4	0.4	0.4	0.7	-	-	-	1.9	1.5
PROPRIETORS, MANAGERS AND OFFICIALS	3.4	0.4	1.1	3.2	4.8	5.9	2.7	-	-	2.6	3.7	6.1
CLERICAL WORKERS	4.8	3.4	5.4	5.8	4.3	3.0	10.3	-	13.5	18.2	3.7	5.1
SALES PERSONS	5.8	9.6	5.2	5.3	5.2	4.7	7.0	-	9.1	5.2	7.4	7.6
TELEPHONE, TELEGRAPH AND RADIO OPERATORS	0.2	-	0.1	0.2	0.4	0.4	2.0	-	1.4	5.2	1.9	-
SKILLED WORKERS	16.6	2.8	9.5	17.6	22.4	24.1	0.3	-	-	-	-	-
SEMI-SKILLED WORKERS	23.8	27.3	29.3	25.6	20.5	14.7	25.9	-	28.4	18.2	27.8	33.3
UNSKILLED WORKERS	33.1	44.5	36.2	29.8	29.3	34.9	2.3	-	-	2.6	5.6	1.5
SERVANTS AND ALLIED WORKERS	10.1	10.5	10.3	9.8	10.5	9.5	42.5	-	41.8	44.1	36.9	39.4
HEADS OF FAMILY GROUPS	100.0	(a)	100.0	100.0	100.0	100.0	100.0	(a)	(a)	100.0	100.0	100.0
PROFESSIONAL PERSONS	3.9	-	1.5	3.9	4.9	4.5	5.1	-	-	2.4	8.6	-
SEMI-PROFESSIONAL AND RECREATIONAL WORKERS	0.5	-	-	0.7	0.3	0.6	-	-	-	-	-	-
PROPRIETORS, MANAGERS, AND OFFICIALS	15.0	-	8.5	10.5	16.2	26.4	3.4	-	-	-	11.4	-
CLERICAL WORKERS	3.5	-	6.0	4.6	2.2	1.6	9.3	-	-	11.9	11.4	7.1
SALES PERSONS	8.1	-	10.9	7.7	7.8	7.1	9.3	-	-	4.8	11.4	10.7
TELEPHONE, TELEGRAPH AND RADIO OPERATORS	0.1	-	-	0.2	-	-	-	-	-	-	-	-
SKILLED WORKERS	20.1	-	11.9	20.7	22.4	22.2	1.7	-	-	2.4	2.9	-
SEMI-SKILLED WORKERS	20.1	-	22.9	23.0	20.7	11.7	27.1	-	-	35.7	17.1	39.4
UNSKILLED WORKERS	22.2	-	33.3	21.9	16.9	21.4	7.6	-	-	4.8	5.7	7.1
SERVANTS AND ALLIED WORKERS	6.5	-	5.0	5.9	8.6	4.5	36.5	-	-	38.0	31.5	35.7

(A) PERCENTAGE NOT COMPUTED BECAUSE OF SMALL NUMBERS INVOLVED.

TABLE 21 DURATION OF LAST JOB AT USUAL OCCUPATION BEFORE MIGRATION, REPORTED BY TRANSIENTS REGISTERED FOR RELIEF IN 13 CITIES, FEBRUARY THROUGH APRIL 1935

DURATION	UNATTACHED PERSONS			HEADS OF FAMILY GROUPS		
	FEBRUARY	MARCH	APRIL	FEBRUARY	MARCH	APRIL
WITH USUAL OCCUPATION BEFORE MIGRATION	15,727	19,682	19,691	1,485	1,541	1,582
			Percent Distribution			
WITH USUAL OCCUPATION BEFORE MIGRATION	100	100	100	100	100	100
UNDER 6 MONTHS	19	18	18	16	17	18
6-17 MONTHS	27	27	28	26	24	24
18-47 MONTHS	29	29	28	25	29	29
4 YEARS AND OVER	24	25	25	32	29	28
NOT ASCERTAINABLE	1	1	1	1	1	1

TABLE 22. DURATION OF FIRST JOB AFTER BEGINNING MIGRATION REPORTED BY TRANSIENTS REGISTERED FOR RELIEF IN 13 CITIES, FEBRUARY THROUGH APRIL 1935

DURATION OF EMPLOYMENT DURING MIGRATION	UNATTACHED PERSONS			HEADS OF FAMILY GROUPS		
	FEBRUARY	MARCH	APRIL	FEBRUARY	MARCH	APRIL
ALL PERSONS	19008	23953	24268	1669	1759	1769
EMPLOYED ON REGISTRATION DAY	41	25	27	21	27	24
NO JOB	12460	16097	16862	943	981	1039
ONE OR MORE JOBS	6507	7831	7379	705	751	706
			Percent Distribution			
ALL PERSONS	100	100	100	100	100	100
EMPLOYED ON REGISTRATION DAY	*	*	*	1	1	1
NO JOB	66	67	70	57	56	59
ONE OR MORE JOBS	34	33	30	42	43	40
DURATION OF FIRST OF ONE OR MORE JOBS	100	100	100	100	100	100
3-14 DAYS	24	23	23	23	22	19
15-30 DAYS	8	8	8	7	7	6
1-2 MONTHS	27	26	27	26	25	26
3-5 MONTHS	20	21	22	24	25	26
6-11 MONTHS	11	11	12	13	13	15
12 MONTHS AND OVER	5	5	5	5	6	6
NOT ASCERTAINABLE	5	6	3	2	2	2

* LESS THAN .5 PERCENT.

TABLE 23A. CASUAL AND NON-CASUAL OCCUPATIONS OF UNATTACHED TRANSIENTS REGISTERED FOR RELIEF IN 13 CITIES, OCTOBER 1934, THROUGH APRIL 1935

Casual and Non-Casual Occupations	1934			1935			
	October	November	December	January	February	March	April
Before beginning migration							
Usual occupation	21,439	19,283	18,056	17,215	15,681	19,539	19,673
			Percent Distribution				
Usual occupation	100	100	100	100	100	100	100
Casual	5	6	6	6	5	5	5
Non-casual	94	93	93	93	95	94	95
Not ascertainable	1	1	1	1	*	1	*
After beginning migration							
One or more jobs	9354	9068	8593	7753	6547	7856	7406
One job only	4869	4780	4488	4123	3451	4137	3962
Two or more jobs	4485	4288	4105	3630	3096	3719	3444
			Percent Distribution				
First of one or more jobs	100	100	100	100	100	100	100
Casual	39	45	44	42	37	38	37
Non-casual	55	53	52	55	58	58	61
Not ascertainable	6	2	4	3	3	4	2
Last of two or more jobs	100	100	100	100	100	100	100
Casual	48	54	50	45	42	42	42
Non-casual	44	45	47	52	56	53	57
Not ascertainable	8	1	3	3	2	5	1

* LESS THAN .5 PERCENT.

TABLE 23B. CASUAL AND NON-CASUAL OCCUPATIONS OF HEADS OF TRANSIENT FAMILY GROUPS REGISTERED FOR RELIEF IN 13 CITIES OCTOBER, 1934, THROUGH APRIL 1935

Casual and Non-Casual Occupations	1934			1935			
	October	November	December	January	February	March	April
Before beginning migration							
Usual occupation	1725	1866	1938	2012	1479	1536	1578
			Percent Distribution				
Usual occupation	100	100	100	100	100	100	100
Casual	3	4	7	6	5	5	4
Non-casual	95	94	92	93	95	94	96
Not ascertainable	2	2	1	1	*	1	*
After beginning migration							
One or more jobs	870	896	1012	1095	726	778	730
One job only	518	582	642	670	443	437	391
Two or more jobs	352	314	370	425	285	341	339
			Percent Distribution				
First of one or more jobs	100	100	100	100	100	100	100
Casual	27	30	33	24	24	26	23
Non-casual	65	67	64	70	75	72	76
Not ascertainable	8	3	3	6	1	2	1
Last of two or more jobs	100	100	100	100	100	100	100
Casual	33	35	38	32	30	29	23
Non-casual	50	60	58	65	58	69	76
Not ascertainable	17	5	4	3	2	2	1

* LESS THAN .5 PERCENT.

TABLE 24A. REASON FOR BEGINNING MIGRATION FOR UNATTACHED TRANSIENTS REGISTERED FOR RELIEF
IN 13 CITIES, OCTOBER 1934, THROUGH APRIL 1935

REASON FOR BEGINNING MIGRATION	1934			1935			
	OCTOBER	NOVEMBER	DECEMBER	JANUARY	FEBRUARY	MARCH	APRIL
UNATTACHED TRANSIENTS	25,160	23,412	21,835	20,613	19,008	23,953	24,268
			Percent Distribution				
UNATTACHED TRANSIENTS	100	100	100	100	100	100	100
SEEKING WORK	69	70	71	72	74	74	75
PROMISED JOB	2	3	2	2	2	2	2
ADVENTURE	8	7	7	7	7	7	8
ILL HEALTH	2	2	2	2	2	2	2
MIGRATORY OCCUPATION	5	5	5	4	3	3	3
DOMESTIC DIFFICULTIES	4	4	4	3	3	3	3
INADEQUATE RELIEF	3	2	2	2	2	2	1
VISITS	4	4	3	4	4	4	4
PERSONAL BUSINESS	1	1	1	1	1	1	1
OTHER REASONS	2	2	2	2	2	1	1
NOT ASCERTAINABLE	*	*	1	1	*	1	*

* LESS THAN .5 PERCENT.

TABLE 24B. REASON FOR BEGINNING MIGRATION FOR HEADS OF TRANSIENT FAMILY GROUPS REGISTERED
FOR RELIEF IN 13 CITIES, OCTOBER 1934, THROUGH APRIL 1935

REASON FOR BEGINNING MIGRATION	1934			1935			
	OCTOBER	NOVEMBER	DECEMBER	JANUARY	FEBRUARY	MARCH	APRIL
HEADS OF TRANSIENT FAMILIES	1,908	2,064	2,137	2,261	1,669	1,759	1,769
			Percent Distribution				
HEADS OF TRANSIENT FAMILIES	100	100	100	100	100	100	100
SEEKING WORK	65	67	66	66	67	65	68
PROMISED JOB	5	6	5	6	4	4	4
ADVENTURE	1	*	1	*	1	1	*
ILL HEALTH	11	10	12	11	11	10	11
MIGRATORY OCCUPATION	3	2	2	3	1	2	2
DOMESTIC DIFFICULTIES	4	2	2	2	3	2	2
INADEQUATE RELIEF	3	3	3	2	4	4	3
VISITS	4	4	4	5	5	5	5
PERSONAL BUSINESS	1	4	2	2	2	2	1
OTHER REASONS	1	1	3	3	2	5	4
NOT ASCERTAINABLE	1	1	*	*	—	*	*

* LESS THAN .5 PERCENT

TABLE 25.   RATE OF ADDITION, AND DURATION OF MIGRATION OF TRANSIENTS REGISTERED FOR RELIEF IN 13
CITIES, OCTOBER 1934, THROUGH APRIL 1935

RATE OF ADDITION AND DURATION OF MIGRATION	1934			1935			
	OCTOBER	NOVEMBER	DECEMBER	JANUARY	FEBRUARY	MARCH	APRIL
UNATTACHED PERSONS REGISTERED	25,160	23,412	21,835	20,613	19,008	23,953	24,268
FAMILY GROUPS REGISTERED	1,908	2,064	2,137	2,261	1,669	1,759	1,769
RATE OF ADDITION, PERCENT[A]							
UNATTACHED PERSONS	19	17	15	18	17	21	20
FAMILY GROUPS	16	13	15	12	11	13	13
DURATION OF MIGRATION				*Percent Distribution*			
UNATTACHED PERSONS	100	100	100	100	100	100	100
6 MONTHS OR LESS	63	61	57	58	58	59	57
7 TO 12 MONTHS	14	16	18	19	19	19	20
1 TO 2 YEARS	6	7	8	7	8	7	8
2 TO 3 YEARS	3	4	4	5	4	4	4
3 TO 4 YEARS	3	3	3	2	2	3	3
4 YEARS AND OVER	10	9	10	9	9	8	8
NOT ASCERTAINABLE	1	*	–	*	*	–	*
FAMILY GROUPS	100	100	100	100	100	100	100
6 MONTHS OR LESS	60	61	56	58	55	53	53
7 TO 12 MONTHS	18	19	22	22	24	26	26
1 TO 2 YEARS	8	8	8	10	9	8	9
2 TO 3 YEARS	3	3	4	5	4	4	3
3 TO 4 YEARS	2	2	2	2	2	2	2
4 YEARS AND OVER	6	7	8	3	6	7	7
NOT ASCERTAINABLE	3	*	*	*	*	*	–

* LESS THAN .5 PERCENT.

A   IN COMPUTING THIS RATE, PERSONS REGISTERING FOR RELIEF WITHIN THE MONTH OF BEGINNING MIGRATION
WERE CONSIDERED AS ADDITIONS TO THE POPULATION DURING THE MONTH; AND THE RATIO OF THESE CASES TO
THE TOTAL NUMBER REGISTERED DURING THE MONTH, EXPRESSED AS PERCENT, IS THE RATE OF ADDITION.

TABLE 26   ORIGIN OF INTERSTATE TRANSIENTS UNDER CARE ON ONE DAY AT THREE MONTH INTERVALS,
SEPTEMBER 30, 1934, TO JUNE 30, 1935, TOTAL UNITED STATES[A]

GEOGRAPHIC DIVISIONS	1930 U.S. CENSUS[B]	UNATTACHED PERSONS				FAMILY GROUPS			
		SEPTEMBER, 30 1934	DECEMBER, 31 1934	MARCH 31 1935	JUNE 30 1935	SEPTEMBER, 30 1934	DECEMBER, 31 1934	MARCH 31 1935	JUNE 30 1935
TOTAL UNITED STATES	122,775,046	104,899	127,901	125,712	102,211	21,186	28,804	30,307	28,919
		Percent Distribution							
TOTAL UNITED STATES	100.0	100.0	100.0	100.0	100.0	100.0	100.0	100.0	100.0
NEW ENGLAND	5.7	6.1	6.3	6.5	5.1	2.9	2.7	2.8	2.5
MIDDLE ATLANTIC	21.4	17.5	17.0	17.0	16.2	11.0	10.3	10.4	9.7
EAST NORTH CENTRAL	20.6	20.3	20.6	20.0	19.0	15.5	15.8	14.7	13.5
WEST NORTH CENTRAL	10.8	10.4	11.7	11.5	10.8	13.2	16.6	17.1	17.2
SOUTH ATLANTIC	12.9	14.8	12.2	12.4	14.0	12.3	13.0	9.9	10.4
EAST SOUTH CENTRAL	8.1	9.1	9.2	9.2	8.7	10.5	9.3	8.6	8.8
WEST SOUTH CENTRAL	9.9	10.1	10.2	10.4	11.9	17.5	18.0	19.6	21.3
MOUNTAIN STATES	3.0	4.6	5.8	5.9	5.3	8.1	9.5	8.9	9.0
PACIFIC STATES	5.7	7.1	8.0	8.1	8.1	8.9	8.8	8.1	7.6

A FROM THE QUARTERLY REPORTS OF THE DIVISION OF TRANSIENT ACTIVITIES.
B FIFTEENTH CENSUS, VOL. 1, TABLE 5. NOTE: THE DISTRIBUTION OF FAMILIES, INCLUDING ONE PERSON
FAMILIES, DOES NOT DIFFER FROM THE DISTRIBUTION OF THE TOTAL POPULATION SHOWN ABOVE BY MORE THAN
0.6 PERCENT IN ANY GEOGRAPHIC DIVISION.

TABLE 27A. ORIGIN OF INTERSTATE TRANSIENTS UNDER CARE ON ONE DAY AT THREE MONTH INTERVALS, SEPTEMBER 30, 1934, TO JUNE 30, 1935, TOTAL UNITED STATES

LAST STATE OF 12 MONTHS' RESIDENCE	UNATTACHED PERSONS				FAMILY GROUPS			
	1934		1935		1934		1935	
	SEPTEMBER	DECEMBER	MARCH	JUNE	SEPTEMBER	DECEMBER	MARCH	JUNE
ALL STATES	104,899	127,801	125,712	102,211	21,186	28,804	30,307	28,919
NEW ENGLAND	6,437	8,066	8,162	6,241	612	764	821	726
MAINE	617	757	802	570	70	81	81	78
NEW HAMPSHIRE	377	540	544	340	25	37	30	19
VERMONT	325	369	386	267	71	81	101	86
MASSACHUSETTS	3,268	4,048	4,161	3,352	274	334	359	284
RHODE ISLAND	744	797	788	620	56	57	50	52
CONNECTICUT	1,106	1,555	1,481	1,092	116	174	200	207
MIDDLE ATLANTIC	18,311	21,768	21,362	16,597	2,320	2,970	3,155	2,792
NEW YORK	8,521	10,513	10,238	7,355	998	1,162	1,243	1,067
NEW JERSEY	2,579	3,312	3,139	2,232	353	558	636	585
PENNSYLVANIA	7,211	7,943	7,985	7,010	969	1,250	1,276	1,140
EAST NORTH CENTRAL	21,352	26,371	25,200	19,376	3,305	4,537	4,471	3,902
OHIO	5,629	7,093	6,175	4,977	804	1,047	951	843
INDIANA	2,735	3,176	3,082	2,223	544	683	730	685
ILLINOIS	6,635	8,306	8,230	6,526	1,007	1,505	1,450	1,257
MICHIGAN	4,628	5,531	5,605	4,064	676	881	942	799
WISCONSIN	1,725	2,265	2,108	1,586	274	421	398	318
WEST NORTH CENTRAL	10,889	15,001	14,412	11,052	2,792	4,789	5,162	4,979
MINNESOTA	1,663	2,442	2,390	1,683	293	400	447	327
IOWA	1,691	2,237	2,083	1,617	375	532	561	487
MISSOURI	3,875	4,777	4,992	3,895	994	1,664	1,718	1,790
NORTH DAKOTA	590	1,024	834	616	122	285	342	290
SOUTH DAKOTA	451	777	732	502	158	333	455	357
NEBRASKA	1,022	1,559	1,489	1,128	335	715	745	709
KANSAS	1,597	2,185	1,932	1,611	515	860	894	1,019
SOUTH ATLANTIC	15,572	15,546	15,537	14,281	2,619	2,900	3,006	3,029
DELAWARE	209	380	393	315	33	49	62	53
MARYLAND	1,505	1,688	1,741	1,303	156	234	230	209
VIRGINIA	2,198	2,265	2,130	1,696	288	358	435	375
WEST VIRGINIA	1,952	2,148	2,274	1,906	269	299	309	341
NORTH CAROLINA	2,457	2,335	2,526	2,425	394	401	434	409
SOUTH CAROLINA	1,615	1,449	1,314	1,507	247	269	290	299
GEORGIA	2,789	2,578	2,478	2,354	667	715	583	690
FLORIDA	2,019	1,757	1,743	2,094	444	438	427	534
DIST. OF COLUMBIA	828	946	938	691	121	137	136	119
EAST SOUTH CENTRAL	9,525	10,415	10,262	8,889	2,214	2,685	2,619	2,549
KENTUCKY	2,576	2,771	2,949	2,284	555	668	623	657
TENNESSEE	2,773	3,016	3,176	2,760	683	805	744	687
ALABAMA	2,627	2,777	2,614	2,352	492	576	581	596
MISSISSIPPI	1,549	1,851	1,523	1,493	484	636	671	609
WEST SOUTH CENTRAL	10,580	12,984	13,102	12,015	3,711	5,187	5,928	6,156
ARKANSAS	1,761	2,299	2,464	2,212	689	1,080	1,115	1,126
LOUISIANA	1,644	1,868	1,730	1,756	358	486	513	504
OKLAHOMA	3,117	3,852	3,637	3,159	1,294	1,897	2,279	2,569
TEXAS	4,058	4,966	5,271	4,888	1,370	1,724	2,019	1,957
MOUNTAIN STATES	4,778	7,391	7,454	5,431	1,718	2,437	2,679	2,601
MONTANA	705	1,323	1,208	793	187	235	284	214
IDAHO	384	647	622	459	219	320	393	327
WYOMING	369	586	591	380	79	205	190	170
COLORADO	1,295	1,903	1,901	1,379	506	655	720	731
NEW MEXICO	411	699	672	563	160	288	296	369
ARIZONA	780	955	960	837	329	446	405	459
UTAH	408	555	551	462	155	193	262	218
NEVADA	426	723	949	558	83	95	129	113
PACIFIC STATES	7,455	10,255	10,221	8,329	1,895	2,535	2,468	2,185
WASHINGTON	1,577	2,436	2,391	1,866	372	583	673	560
OREGON	988	1,688	1,688	1,256	406	521	494	475
CALIFORNIA	4,890	6,135	6,142	5,207	1,117	1,431	1,301	1,150

TABLE 278. (PERCENT DISTRIBUTION) ORIGIN OF INTERSTATE TRANSIENTS UNDER CARE ON ONE DAY AT THREE MONTH INTERVALS, SEPTEMBER 30, 1934, TO JUNE 30, 1935, TOTAL UNITED STATES

LAST STATE OF 12 MONTHS' RESIDENCE	UNATTACHED PERSONS				FAMILY GROUPS			
	1934		1935		1934		1935	
	SEPTEMBER	DECEMBER	MARCH	JUNE	SEPTEMBER	DECEMBER	MARCH	JUNE
ALL STATES	100.0	100.0	100.0	100.0	100.0	100.0	100.0	100.0
NEW ENGLAND	6.1	6.3	6.5	6.1	2.9	2.7	2.8	2.5
MAINE	0.6	0.6	0.6	0.5	0.3	0.3	0.3	0.3
NEW HAMPSHIRE	0.4	0.4	0.4	0.3	0.1	0.1	0.1	0.1
VERMONT	0.3	0.3	0.3	0.3	0.3	0.3	0.3	0.2
MASSACHUSETTS	3.1	3.2	3.4	3.3	1.3	1.2	1.2	1.0
RHODE ISLAND	0.7	0.6	0.6	0.6	0.3	0.2	0.2	0.2
CONNECTICUT	1.0	1.2	1.2	1.1	0.6	0.6	0.7	0.7
MIDDLE ATLANTIC	17.5	17.0	17.0	16.2	11.0	10.3	10.4	9.7
NEW YORK	8.1	8.2	8.1	7.1	4.7	4.0	4.1	3.7
NEW JERSEY	2.5	2.6	2.5	2.2	1.7	2.0	2.1	2.0
PENNSYLVANIA	6.9	6.2	6.4	6.9	4.6	4.3	4.2	4.0
EAST NORTH CENTRAL	20.3	20.6	20.0	19.0	15.6	15.8	14.7	13.5
OHIO	5.4	5.5	4.9	4.9	3.8	3.6	3.1	2.9
INDIANA	2.6	2.5	2.4	2.2	2.6	2.4	2.4	2.4
ILLINOIS	6.3	6.5	6.5	6.3	4.7	5.2	4.9	4.3
MICHIGAN	4.4	4.3	4.5	4.0	3.2	3.1	3.1	2.8
WISCONSIN	1.6	1.8	1.7	1.6	1.3	1.5	1.3	1.1
WEST NORTH CENTRAL	10.4	11.7	11.5	10.8	13.2	16.6	17.1	17.2
MINNESOTA	1.6	1.9	1.9	1.5	1.4	1.4	1.5	1.1
IOWA	1.6	1.8	1.5	1.6	1.8	1.8	1.9	1.7
MISSOURI	3.7	3.7	4.0	3.8	4.7	5.8	5.7	6.2
NORTH DAKOTA	0.5	0.8	0.7	0.6	0.6	1.0	1.1	1.0
SOUTH DAKOTA	0.4	0.6	0.6	0.5	0.7	1.2	1.5	1.2
NEBRASKA	1.0	1.2	1.2	1.1	1.6	2.4	2.5	2.5
KANSAS	1.5	1.7	1.5	1.6	2.4	3.0	2.9	3.5
SOUTH ATLANTIC	14.9	12.2	12.4	14.0	12.3	10.0	9.9	10.4
DELAWARE	0.2	0.3	0.3	0.3	0.2	0.2	0.2	0.2
MARYLAND	1.4	1.3	1.4	1.3	0.7	0.9	0.8	0.7
VIRGINIA	2.1	1.8	1.7	1.5	1.4	1.2	1.4	1.3
WEST VIRGINIA	1.9	1.7	1.8	1.9	1.3	1.0	1.0	1.2
NORTH CAROLINA	2.3	1.8	2.0	2.4	1.8	1.4	1.4	1.4
SOUTH CAROLINA	1.5	1.1	1.1	1.5	1.2	0.9	1.0	1.0
GEORGIA	2.7	2.0	2.0	2.3	3.1	2.5	2.3	2.4
FLORIDA	1.9	1.4	1.4	2.0	2.0	1.5	1.4	1.8
DIST. OF COLUMBIA	0.8	0.8	0.7	0.7	0.6	0.5	0.4	0.4
EAST SOUTH CENTRAL	9.1	9.2	9.2	8.7	10.5	9.3	8.6	8.8
KENTUCKY	2.5	2.2	2.4	2.2	2.6	2.3	2.1	2.3
TENNESSEE	2.6	2.3	2.5	2.7	3.3	2.8	2.4	2.3
ALABAMA	2.5	2.2	2.1	2.3	2.3	2.0	1.9	2.1
MISSISSIPPI	1.5	1.5	1.2	1.5	2.3	2.2	2.2	2.1
WEST SOUTH CENTRAL	10.1	10.2	10.4	11.8	17.5	18.0	19.6	21.3
ARKANSAS	1.7	1.8	2.0	2.2	3.3	3.7	3.7	3.9
LOUISIANA	1.6	1.5	1.4	1.7	1.7	1.7	1.7	1.7
OKLAHOMA	3.0	3.0	2.9	3.1	6.1	5.6	7.5	8.9
TEXAS	3.8	3.9	4.1	4.8	6.4	6.0	6.7	6.8
MOUNTAIN STATES	4.6	5.8	5.9	5.3	9.1	9.5	9.8	9.0
MONTANA	0.7	1.0	1.0	0.8	0.9	0.8	0.9	0.7
IDAHO	0.4	0.5	0.5	0.4	1.0	1.1	1.3	1.1
WYOMING	0.4	0.5	0.5	0.4	0.4	0.7	0.6	0.5
COLORADO	1.2	1.5	1.5	1.3	2.4	2.3	2.4	2.5
NEW MEXICO	0.4	0.5	0.5	0.6	0.7	1.0	1.0	1.3
ARIZONA	0.7	0.8	0.8	0.8	1.5	1.6	1.3	1.6
UTAH	0.4	0.4	0.4	0.5	0.7	0.7	0.9	0.9
NEVADA	0.4	0.6	0.7	0.5	0.4	0.3	0.4	0.4
PACIFIC STATES	7.1	8.0	8.1	9.1	8.9	8.8	9.1	7.6
WASHINGTON	1.5	1.9	1.9	1.8	1.8	2.0	2.2	1.9
OREGON	0.9	1.3	1.3	1.2	1.9	1.8	1.6	1.7
CALIFORNIA	4.7	4.8	4.9	5.1	5.2	5.0	4.3	4.0

TABLE 28. ORIGIN, BY RURAL AND URBAN AREAS, OF UNATTACHED AND FAMILY GROUP TRANSIENTS REGISTERED FOR RELIEF IN 13 CITIES, NOVEMBER 1934, THROUGH APRIL 1935

SIZE OF PLACE	1934		1935			
	NOVEMBER	DECEMBER	JANUARY	FEBRUARY	MARCH	APRIL
UNATTACHED PERSONS	23,412	21,835	20,613	19,008	23,953	24,268
FAMILY GROUPS	2,064	2,137	2,261	1,669	1,759	1,769
			Percent Distribution			
UNATTACHED PERSONS	100.0	100.0	100.0	100.0	100.0	100.0
RURAL	20.1	20.1	20.5	20.1	20.1	21.1
FARM AND OPEN COUNTRY	5.7	6.2	7.1	7.1	7.5	7.6
TOWNS UNDER 2,500	13.4	13.9	13.4	13.0	12.5	13.5
URBAN[A]	79.6	79.4	79.0	79.5	79.0	78.6
NOT ASCERTAINABLE	0.3	0.5	0.5	0.4	0.9	0.3
FAMILY GROUPS	100.0	100.0	100.0	100.0	100.0	100.0
RURAL	30.5	29.9	26.6	26.4	26.4	27.7
FARM AND OPEN COUNTRY	9.7	8.5	7.6	9.4	7.9	9.3
TOWNS UNDER 2,500	20.8	21.4	19.0	17.0	18.5	18.4
URBAN[A]	69.0	69.3	72.6	73.2	72.8	71.7
NOT ASCERTAINABLE	0.5	0.8	0.8	0.4	0.8	0.6

A PLACES WITH 2,500 OR MORE POPULATION IN 1930.

TABLE 29. ORIGIN OF MIGRATION BY SIZE OF PLACE, UNATTACHED AND FAMILY GROUP TRANSIENTS REGISTERED FOR RELIEF IN 13 CITIES, FOR SELECTED MONTHS

SIZE OF PLACE	UNATTACHED PERSONS				FAMILY GROUPS			
	1934		1935		1934		1935	
	NOVEMBER	DECEMBER	MARCH	APRIL	NOVEMBER	DECEMBER	MARCH	APRIL
ALL PERSONS	23,412	21,835	23,953	24,268	2,064	2,137	1,759	1,769
				Percent Distribution				
ALL PERSONS	100.0	100.0	100.0	100.0	100.0	100.0	100.0	100.0
RURAL	20.1	20.1	20.1	21.1	30.5	29.9	26.4	27.7
FARM AND OPEN COUNTRY	6.7	6.2	7.5	7.6	9.7	8.5	7.9	9.3
TOWNS UNDER 2,500	13.4	13.9	12.6	13.5	20.8	21.4	18.5	18.4
URBAN	79.3	79.1	78.9	78.4	69.0	69.3	72.8	71.7
2,500 TO 10,000	9.9	10.0	10.2	10.4	12.3	12.2	12.1	13.6
10,000 TO 25,000	8.3	8.2	7.8	8.2	8.4	8.5	9.8	8.6
25,000 TO 50,000	6.6	6.6	6.9	7.0	6.0	6.8	6.6	6.9
50,000 TO 100,000	6.6	6.7	6.9	6.8	6.9	5.3	8.4	7.4
100,000 AND OVER	47.9	47.6	47.1	46.0	35.4	36.5	35.9	35.2
NOT ASCERTAINABLE	0.6	0.8	1.0	0.5	0.5	0.8	0.8	0.6

APPENDIX C

Case History Abstracts

This appendix presents reasons for beginning migration in more detail than is possible in tabular form. The details were abstracted from selected case histories of unattached persons and heads of family groups registered for relief at transient bureaus. The case histories selected for abstract were chosen to illustrate the several reasons for migration listed in tables Tables 24a and 24b, Appendix B.

Seeking Work

Case No. 1. Steve P- , age thirty-eight, was born in rural West Virginia. He was taken out of school at the age of fourteen and put to work in a coal mine. He disliked the unpleasant and difficult work in the mines, but had neither the money to leave nor the training to change employment. By 1917 he quit the mines to serve in the Army, and extended his stay by reenlisting at the termination of the War.

In 1922 he returned to West Virginia, married, and resumed work in the coal mines. He continued this employment for ten years; but, because of the frequent shut-down of the mines, he was unable to provide his family with anything but the barest necessities of life.

After months of unemployment in 1932 and 1933, Mr. P- obtained for the family a small relief allowance which, because of its regularity, enabled them to live more comfortably than they had in years.

With his family provided for, Mr. P- set out in search of work. His only concern was that the work be in some industry other than mining, and that he could move his family out of West Virginia. At the time he was registered at the Denver Colorado transient bureau, Mr. P- had traveled by freight over the entire Southwest and Pacific Coast. During his travels he had obtained short-time work as harvest hand, unskilled laborer on construction work, and as a fish cannery worker. None of these jobs lasted more than a month.

Mr. P- asked to be allowed to remain in the Denver transient bureau until he had explored the employment possibilities of that area.

Case No. 2. Joseph M- , age forty-one, had worked for twenty years as a repairman in a Wisconsin railroad shop. In 1929 he had saved enough money to purchase a farm in Ashland County, Wisconsin, to which he moved his wife and nine children. Unable to meet the mortgage payments, the M's lost the farm and rented a small tract of land, which they operated as a truck garden. This project failed because of the small money return for their produce; and in 1934 the family possessions were reduced to farm tools and an old truck.

A friend of Mrs. M- in the State of Washington wrote that conditions were much better on the Pacific Coast, and encouraged the family to come there. Mr. M- made a trip to Washington by truck, and started negotiations to take over some farm land. He then returned for family and tools. The trip to Washington was made by truck. At Seattle the family was forced to apply for aid from the transient bureau until they could take possession of the farm land.

The Seattle transient bureau agreed to take care of the family until the farm could be occupied. The prospects of the family's becoming self-supporting were considered good, since Mr. M- believed he could cut and sell enough timber from the farm land to finance their first year's operations.

The registration of the family group at the Seattle transient bureau was the first time they had applied for relief.

Case No. 3. Ralph D- , age twenty, was one of five children of an Arkansas share-chopper. His schooling had not extended beyond the third year of grade school, largely because of the necessity of helping with the farm work. The family was extremely poor, and as long as Ralph could remember had been in debt to the owners of the land or to the general store from which they obtained their supplies.

Whenever possible, the boy "hired out" on one of the neighboring farms to supplement the family earnings. In 1932 the D- family not only made no money but were refused further credit at the store and threatened with eviction.

At this point, Ralph set out to find work in some other farming area in the hope that he could earn enough to send money to his family.

He had been away from home for two years when he was registered for relief at the Dallas Texas transient bureau. During his wanderings he had secured enough work to support himself most of the time, but had been unable to send any money home.

He asked the Dallas transient bureau to make inquiry about his family, from whom he had received no word during his wandering. The transient bureau arranged for his stay in the transient bureau shelter until word was received from Arkansas.

Case No. 4. William S- , age fifty-nine, and his wife, age fifty, had lived many years in a small town in Illinois where Mr. S- was employed as a baker. His earnings had been sufficient to allow saving part of his wages each week for a number of years; and when, in 1931, he lost his job, Mr. and Mrs. S- were not particularly concerned for the immediate future.

However, in 1932, the bank in which their savings were deposited was closed, and in the subsequent liquidation, Mr. S- received only a small part of his savings. When this money was gone and it was apparent that no work was to be had in the town in which they had lived most of their lives, the S- fam-

ily decided to go to Kansas City, Missouri, where Mr. S- thought
he might find work at his trade.

The S- family lived in Kansas City for nearly three years
without applying for relief. When they were finally reduced
to destitution and made application, they were unable to obtain relief as residents of Kansas City because they had maintained their legal settlement in the Illinois community. As a
result they were referred to the Kansas City transient bureau.

The transient bureau officials felt that Mr. S- was unemployable because of his age and his health, which had been impaired
by the years of worry and privation. Therefore, the transient
bureau was planning to return the family to Illinois, where
they had legal settlement.

Case No. 5. Charley C- , age sixty-one, an American-born
Chinese, had been employed most of his life as a waiter in
Chinese restaurants in Denver, Colorado. He had held his last
job, which was terminated by the closing of the restaurant, for
fifteen years.

Unable to find further employment in Denver, Mr. C- , with
his 31-year-old wife and five children, ranging in age from 4
to 12 years, returned to San Francisco, his birthplace, where
he had heard employment conditions were better.

After an unsuccessful search for work in San Francisco,
Mr. C- , his funds exhausted, applied for relief at the transient bureau. He was determined to remain in San Francisco,
where the family might live in the Chinese colony and the children attend school.

The family had been at the San Francisco transient bureau
six months at the time this abstract was made. This was their
first time on relief.

Promised Job

Case No. 6. James M- , age twenty-two, lived with his parents in St. Louis, Missouri. Early in 1935 he lost his job in
a pharmacy and was unable to find employment of any kind. His
brother was a chain-store manager in San Francisco, and wrote
that he could obtain a job for James in one of the company's
stores. James M- made the trip to San Francisco by hitch-hiking
and by freight train. When he arrived there, the promised
job could not be obtained. He remained at the home of his
brother until a quarrel caused him to leave.

He decided to go to Los Angeles before returning home,
principally to see the southern part of the State. He had been
at the Los Angeles transient bureau a week when this abstract
was made. James M- planned to leave in a few days and return
to St. Louis over the southern route, by freight train.

Case No. 7.   Edward P- , age thirty-four, had lived most of his life in Brooklyn, New York, where he followed his trade of furniture upholsterer. His last employment at this work lasted for five years, and terminated in the summer of 1934.

Mr. P- remained in Brooklyn for several months after the loss of his job, trying to find work at his trade, but without success. Meanwhile, friends in California had written him that the furniture business was "looking up" in Los Angeles, and that an expert upholsterer could readily obtain employment.

While Mr. P- was considering a move to Los Angeles, he received a letter from his former employer, who had gone to Los Angeles and was working as a foreman in an upholstering plant, promising him a job if he would come to Los Angeles. Mr. P- decided to go, particularly because his wife was in poor health and had been advised that the California climate would be beneficial.

The P- family used their last resources in migrating to Los Angeles.   When they arrived there, they found conditions in the upholstering trade had changed and that the promise of a job could not be fulfilled. They registered for relief at the Los Angeles transient bureau and requested transportation back to Brooklyn.

No final disposition had been made of this case at the time this abstract was made.

Adventure

Case No. 8. Charles H- , age twenty-four, from New England, was graduated from a small college in the spring of 1931. He obtained a position in the accounting department of a large New York corporation at twenty-four dollars a week. In 1932 he was included in a wholesale lay-off of clerks, and remained in New York looking for work until his small savings were exhausted.   He returned to his parents; but after a few months became so restless at the enforced dependency that he borrowed enough money from his father to return to New York to look for work.   When he found it impossible to obtain any form of employment, his pride would not let him return to his parents and dependency a second time.

Convinced that New York City held no possibility of employment for him, Charles H- used his remaining funds to get to Chicago, where the Century of Progress exercised a double attraction—the widely publicized exhibits, and the possibility of obtaining employment where so much was happening.

When he arrived in Chicago, he found that he was one of thousands who had come for much the same reason. Unable to find work, and quickly reduced to destitution, he was about to

ask that word be sent to his parents when he made the acquain-
ance of a boy who had been on the road for about six months,
and who offered to take Charles H- with him on a trip to California.

In the next eighteen months Charles H- traveled back and
forth across the western and southwestern States, his route
determined by curiosity, rumors, and chance companions. Occasionally he found work for short periods of time, but his
clothes became so worn that he was refused consideration on
sight. Gradually he came to depend upon transient centers and
camps for food, shelter, and clothes. He traveled under an
assumed name, gave a fictitious home address, and never stayed
long enough in any place to allow the Transient Relief officials
to investigate his story. His reason for this was that he
feared he might be identified, and that his parents would be
notified.

In the spring of 1935 he obtained permanent employment
through one of the transient bureaus; and, after working about
six months, notified his parents of his whereabouts and apparently resumed a stable way of living.

III Health

Case No. 9.   Albert W- , age twenty-five, had worked most
of his life in the lead and zinc mines of Oklahoma. Mr. W- ,
his wife, age twenty-one, and their four children, ranging in
age from two to six years, lived with Mr. W''s father, who owned
a home. When employment in the mines became uncertain as a
result of decreased mining activity and labor troubles, the
family did not find it necessary to apply for relief. The
father suffered from lung trouble, and as his health grew worse,
an immediate removel to Arizona was advised, necessitating the
sale of the home. Mr. W- decided that the whole family would
go; and in 1933, the journey was made in an old automobile
bought with part of the money realized in the sale of the
house.

In Arizona, the father purchased a horse and wagon, which
enabled Mr. W- to set up a small hauling and junk business, and
support the family until his father's death. Their reserve
funds were exhausted by medical and funeral expenses; and business conditions were so bad that Mr. W- applied for relief,
receiving $3.50 a week. Mr. W- was unwilling to return to
Oklahoma, and hoped the transient bureau would continue to
help him until business picked up. The transient bureau had
been carrying the case for nearly a year at the time of this
abstract.

Migratory Occupation

Case No. 10. Stanley McK- , age twenty-seven, of Texas, was left an orphan at the age of four, and placed in a Masonic home, He stayed at the home until he was seventeen years of age, which was the age limit for inmates. During his stay in the home he had attended school, and had completed the first year of high school. His first employment after leaving the home was with an ice manufacturer and this employment lasted seven months. He then became apprenticed to a boiler maker for a period of two years.

With the advent of the depression, Mr. McK- was laid off; and the only work he could find was with a carnival troupe that toured the Mississippi Valley States.

For several years Mr. McK- worked each spring and summer with one or another carnival company, and came to depend on this type of employment. The wages were not large; but he felt assured of work for the duration of the carnival season.

During the winter of 1934 Mr. McK's savings were insufficient to support him until the carnival started the 1935 season, and he applied for assistance at the Memphis transient bureau. Through the interest of the bureau officials, Mr. McK- attended a trade school during the winter and showed considerable aptitude at mechanical trades. At the time this abstract was made the transient bureau was endeavoring to obtain permanent employment for Mr. McK- , who, however, thought he would join a carnival troupe again as soon as the season opened.

Case No. 11. Mrs. Bertha W- , age forty, a widow, was the head of a family group consisting of four young children, an aged mother, and herself. The family group was originally from Newark, Arkansas, where the husband (deceased) had been a sharecropper, but for the last five years had moved around the country working at the harvesting of various specialty crops. Mr. and Mrs. W- , their eldest daughter, age thirteen, and Mrs. W's mother had all worked at harvesting cotton, grain, and fruit. The direction of the family's many migrations throughout the West and Southwest was largely determined by the maturing of crops. They worked on truck farms in California and Arizona, picked fruit, berries, and cotton in Arkansas and Texas, and worked in the potato fields of Missouri. The family earned enough during the harvest periods to carry them through the off-seasons.

After the death of Mr. W- , the family was unable to follow the customary itinerary, and their earnings dropped below what was needed for subsistence. As a result, they applied for relief at the Phoenix, Arizona, transient bureau, where they had been for about two months at the time this abstract was made.

Case No. 12. Clyde P-, age twenty-two, left home when he

was 16, to go to sea.   He was tired of school and life in his Oklahoma farm home.   He made his way by freight train to Port Arthur, Texas, where he "signed on" as a mess boy on a coast-wise steamer.

For several years he had fairly steady employment. He ship-ped as an ordinary seaman until 1933, when he attained the rating of able-bodied seaman.   His earnings were sufficient to carry him through occasional periods of unemployment.   He us-ually made his headquarters in New York City, where he lived at the Seamen's Church Institute.

In April, 1934, Clyde P- was in Boston without a job.   It had become almost impossible to ship out of New York City be-cause of the depressed condition of the shipping industry; and he had moved from port to port in the hope of finding work.   A Boston relief agency referred him to the transient bureau, where he had been for a month at the time this abstract was made.

Clyde P- had no idea of giving up his regular occupation at sea, and looked for work each day along the Boston water front. He thought that if work could not be found within a short time, he would ride the freight trains to Oklahoma and visit his par-ents before returning to New York City or Baltimore to resume his search for work.

Case No. 13.   Joseph K- , age thirty-eight, had been a sail-or for nearly twenty years when, in 1931, he married and quit the sea for a job in a shoe factory in New England.   He soon tired of this work;   and in 1932 obtained employment with a shipping concern engaged in coastwise traffic. This employment continued until June, 1935, when Mr. K- was laid off.

With a wife and two children to support, Mr. K- had been unable to accumulate any reserve funds. For a month the family lived on Mrs. K's earnings as a part-time domestic servant.

Mr. K- heard that there was a shortage of seamen in Boston; and he and his family "hitch-hiked" their way there, but Mr. K- could not obtain employment.

The family applied for relief at the Boston transient bureau, which agreed to care for the family while Mr. K- continued to look for work.

Domestic Difficulties

Case No. 14.   James N- , age twenty-seven, a native of Rhode Island, attended the Agricultural College of his native State, and became a trained nurseryman.   After leaving college he worked as a tree surgeon in different parts of the country, served a three-year enlistment in the Army, and in 1931 estab-lished a plant and tree nursery in Maine on money borrowed from his mother. Mr. N- married, and was successful in a mod-est way with his business until 1934, when his wife divorced him.

Depressed and restless, Mr. N- sold his nursery and started for California with the idea of starting a tree nursery there. His funds were insufficient for this purpose, and he drifted about the country working as a tree surgeon when work could be found. Occasionally he stopped at transient bureaus over night, but preferred to stop at a farm house and work for his food and lodging. In April, 1935, he stayed a few days at the Memphis transient bureau, where this abstract was made. At that time Mr. N- was en route to California, hoping to obtain backing for a tree nursery.

Case No. 15. Wallace C- , age thirty-two, and his wife, age twenty-seven, were life-long residents of Illinois. They were married in 1928, and Mr. C- rented a farm from his mother-in-law, which he operated until the summer of 1934.

A series of poor crops and the total destruction of one by fire were given by Mr. C- as the reasons for deserting his wife and two children in 1934.

Later his wife and children followed him, and a reconciliation was effected. But the mother-in-law refused to let the family return to the farm as long as the husband was part of the family group.

Mr. C- took his family with him to Nebraska, where he had relatives, hoping to find work in the grain fields.

When no work was to be had, the family went to Florida for the winter, although they had no clear idea as to what they would do there. They stopped at transient bureaus along the way, and had been receiving relief from a Florida transient bureau for nearly a year when the abstract was made.

The bureau planned to place Mr. C- on a Public Works Administration project.

Case No. 16. Billy J- , who was only fifteen years of age, had left his father's farm in northern Oregon after a quarrel that climaxed a long period of antagonism between him and his step-mother. After wandering throughout Oregon and California, Billy applied for aid at the Los Angeles transient bureau.

He had been away from home only a little over a month and boasted of riding freight trains, and living in hobo "jungles" and the transient bureaus. He had enjoyed his short period on the road, and seemed to think transiency was much to be preferred to his life at home. He steadfastly refused to be returned home, stating that it would do no good, and that he would leave again at the first opportunity.

Through relief workers in Oregon, the Los Angeles bureau got in touch with Billy's father, who offered to pay the cost of returning his son. The father stated that Billy presented no problem except in his defiance of his step-mother. Arrangements were made with an aunt to take Billy into her home for a

time, an arrangement that overcame the boy's objection to being sent home.

At the time this abstract was made, the Los Angeles transient bureau was arranging for Billy's transportation to the
home of the aunt.

Inadequate Relief

Case No. 17.   John B- , age twenty-one, of Georgia, was referred to the Miami transient bureau by the police station where
he applied for food and shelter.   He had come to Miami in the
hope of obtaining employment during the winter in one of the
winter resort hotels.

Mr. B- had left his father's farm in Georgia because "there
was no future in farming", and had worked for a time as a ma-
chine tender in a cotton mill, and as a bell-boy in a small
hotel.   In the fall of 1934 he was out of work and unable to
pay his room rent.   He wrote his father asking permission to
return to the farm but was told not to come.   Mr. B- then applied for local relief, hoping to be assigned to a work relief
project.   He claims that he was refused relief because he was
"single and could look out for himself."

At this point he decided to go to Florida where he heard
the large resort hotels were in need of personnel.   After an
unsuccessful search for work in Palm Beach and Miami, he applied for assistance at the Miami police station, apparently
not knowing of the transient relief bureaus.

No disposition had been made of his case at the time this
abstract was made.

Case No. 18.   Jackson S- , age forty-seven, a steam fitter
by trade, lived with his wife and three children in Birmingham,
Alabama, from 1926 until 1935. He had fairly steady employment
with one of the Birmingham steel mills until the spring of 1935,
when the company shut down three of its five furnaces.   Mr. S-
was put on part-time employment, averaging less than five dollars a week in wages.   The family had no other source of income, and applied to the E.R.A. for assistance. Mr. S- claimed
he was refused relief because he had some income.   When the
part-time employment stopped he reapplied for relief, and
claims he was allotted three dollars weekly.

After a vain attempt to supplement this inadequate income,
the head of the family decided that they had nothing to lose
by going on the road. The family hitch-hiked to Augusta, Georgia, where Mr. S- had heard that he might find employment in
the cotton mills. Unable to find work there, they remained at
the transient bureau until it closed.   They started then for
Memphis, Tennessee, but could give no particular reason for
selecting that destination.   En route, the head of the family

obtained two weeks' work in a lumber camp.

When they arrived at Memphis, they registered at the transient bureau, where they were at the time this abstract was made.

Visits

Case No. 19. Robert S- , age twenty, was born in the State of Idaho. His mother died when he was a boy, and he was cared for by his father, who was an itinerant carpenter. At the age of fourteen he left his father, hitch-hiked to Philadelphia, where he supported himself by a series of employments that included selling newspapers, working in a printing shop, delivering telegrams, and working as a stock clerk in a store. During this period he continued his schooling and obtained a high school diploma, of which he was very proud.

In 1934 he went to Seattle, Washington, in search of an uncle who had once offered him a home. Unable to locate the uncle, he returned to the East seeking work, traveling by freight train, and stopping at transient bureaus and Salvation Army shelters. When he reached Philadelphia he could find no work, and continued his wanderings to Boston, where he was staying at the transient bureau when this abstract was made.

Case No. 20. Mrs. Vera J- , age twenty-three, colored, of Texas, with a son, age four, and a daughter, age two, registered for relief at the Chicago transient bureau. Mrs. J- had been separated for more than a year from her husband who, after separation, gave up his job in Houston, Texas, to avoid contributing to the support of his family.

Mrs. J- was employed in Houston, and earned enough to support herself and children. She received word from Chicago that her mother was critically ill, and wanted to see her. Mrs. J- spent what money she had saved for train fare for herself and children to Chicago. When she arrived there, she found that her mother had died. Without funds or friends, Mrs. J- had to apply to the Chicago transient bureau for aid. The transient bureau wanted to return the family to Houston, but Mrs. J- would not agree, because she felt that a colored person in her position would have a better opportunity to reestablish herself in a Northern city. The transient bureau agreed to care for the family for a few weeks in order to give Mrs. J- an opportunity to look for employment.

No disposition of this case had been made at the time of abstract.

Personal Business

Case No. 21. Mrs. Martha F- , age forty-six, had operated a beauty parlor in Detroit, Michigan, for a number of years

following a divorce from her husband.   Upon the death of her
father in Texas,   she sold the shop and went to live in the
home left by her father.   During the depression she was unable
to keep up the mortgage on the home,   and sold her interest in
the property. With the proceeds she went to Miami, Florida, to
open a beauty parlor.

Her funds were insufficient for this purpose, and for a time
she supported herself by making and marketing a face lotion.
When the venture failed she was completely out of funds and
was referred to the Miami transient bureau as a non-resident.
The bureau had considerable difficulty with Mrs. F- , who objected to being placed in a women's shelter.   Meanwhile the
bureau verified Mrs. F's claim to legal settlement, and planned
to send her there.   Mrs. F- refused to go; and the bureau discontinued relief.

Case No. 22.   George L- , age seventy, Swedish-born natural-
ized citizen, had spent most of his active years in engineering
and construction work.   In 1926 he and his wife opened a tourist
home and rooming house in Butte, Montana, which operated until
1929,   when declining business forced them to close the house.
Mr. L- had a piece of property near the area taken over as the
Glacier National Park. The establishment of the Park adversely
affected the value of his land, and he was promised compensation
for his loss.   He and his wife, age seventy-one, remained in
Butte awaiting payment for his property until their resources
were exhausted.   They then set out for Washington, D. C., in
the hope of obtaining something on their alleged claim against
the Government.   Arrived in Washington, they applied for relief at the transient bureau.

Their case history did not show any record of transient or
resident relief prior to their stay at the Washington transient
bureau.

No disposition had been made of their case at the time this
abstract was made.